THE TAILL OF RAUF COILȜEAR

The Scottish Text Society
Fifth Series
no. 16

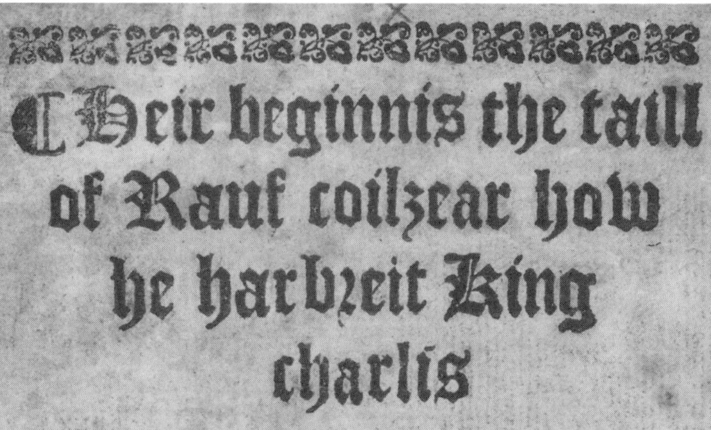
Heir beginnis the taill of Rauf coilȝear how he harbreit King charlis

Imprentit at Sanctandrois be Robert Lekpreuik, Anno, 1572.

NLS H.29.c.9, title page of *The Taill of Rauf Coilȝear*.
By kind permission of the National Library of Scotland, Edinburgh

THE TAILL OF RAUF COILȜEAR

Edited by
Ralph Hanna

The Scottish Text Society

2019

First published 2019 by The Scottish Text Society, Edinburgh

ISBN 978–1–89797–637–1

A Scottish Text Society publication
Published by The Boydell Press
an imprint of Boydell & Brewer Ltd
PO Box 9, Woodbridge, Suffolk IP12 3DF, UK
and of Boydell & Brewer Inc.
668 Mt Hope Avenue, Rochester, NY 14620–2731, USA
website: www.boydellandbrewer.com

A CIP catalogue record for this book is available from the British Library

This publication is printed on acid-free paper

Typeset by
www.thewordservice.com

Printed and bound in Great Britain by
TJ International Ltd, Padstow, Cornwall

Contents

Preface

This volume rounds off a fifty-year project I never had any intention of undertaking, much less bringing to conclusion. I began my research work, on the border-romance *The Awntyrs off Arthure*, in the summer of 1965; this effort introduced me to the grand F. J. Amours and his STS volumes of 1892 and 1897. I had produced an edition of this brief poem a year thence (although it took a good deal longer to get it revised and eventually published). My further engagement with Scots alliterative tradition was rather accidental: around 2000, in concert with Sally Mapstone, now Principal of the University of St Andrews but then at Oxford, I wrested W. R. J. Barron's edition of *Golagros and Gawane*, away from the Early English Text Society which had foolishly accepted it as their own in the late 1980s, for the STS. When Barron unfortunately passed away, leaving the text incomplete, I again responded to the Principal's call and brought his files into a state worthy of STS publication. And thought I was again free for other, non-Caledonian projects.

But the Principal is, like me, a terrier, and she has, down the years, continued to harass me about the remaining poems Amours presented. (One of these, not Scots, had been well served in the interim, first, rather ebulliently by one of my graduate mentors, Sunny Miskimin; more soberly by my friend, the *magister rhythmorum initialium*, Thorlac Turville-Petre.) Sally's act of toleration – at one point, she commented to me that 'you do pretty well with Scots for a Middle English person' – again bore fruit, coerced me out of what I had thought a retirement from such matters. So I made a further interposition, this time with Holland's *Buke of the Howlat*. Yet I had steadfastly refused to touch the remaining poem Amours had presented, *Rauf Coilȝear*, in the belief (although as the Introduction will show, for the wrong reasons) the text was too shabbily transmitted to do a great deal with.

Accident brings me back, for the last time, I imagine. In December 2015, I stumbled across a copy of Beattie's facsimile of Robert Lekpreuik's print in a bookshop and reread the text. This led – Christmas breaks with closed libraries are dangerous to scholarly health – to revivified interest in the text, a developing sense of its dextrous cleverness, and a rather provisional transcription and even more fragmentary glossary. All which I left inert in the computer. But beyond her own prodigious talents, Principal Sally has trained up a new generation of STS mirmydons of considerable suasive power. In the course of generous visits each arranged to their home turfs in spring 2017, the not so gentle prodding of Nicola Royan and Rhiannon Purdie convinced me that I might dust off and formalise the files I had – and bring this accidental project to an end.

Amours was, of course, not alone in his enthusiasm for the poem. In the (post)modern context where even work of the 1990s is too often viewed as superseded and to be ignored, one should insist on the antiquity of scholarly interest in *Rauf Coilȝear*, for the essential parameters of discussion were developed and extensively, if not always critically, discussed in the 1880s and 1890s. In addition to Amours, one must first mention Dickson and Edmond, who managed to gather just about all we know about early Scots printing. But of equal vintage are studies absolutely basic to this poem: Herrtage's careful unpacking of its debt to Charlemagne tradition, Child's extensive discussion of 'the king in disguise' ballads, Tonndorf's linguistic analysis, and Browne's unusually thoughtful textual work. Beyond my debts to them, I would also acknowledge two more recent scholars who, in various ways, have kept both mine and a far larger scholarly community's interest in *Rauf Coilȝear* and related materials alive, my California colleagues old and new, the late Sr Betsy Ross and Stephen Shepherd.

My other debts are considerably more immediate: first, of course, to Sally for her persistence, then to others associated with STS and the production of this volume. Nicola and Rhiannon have, of course, been uniformly helpful in both their interest and their suggestions, and Jeremy Smith has offered trenchant commentary on an earlier draft of these materials. Finally, the Society's publishers, Boydell & Brewer, have converted dodgy computer files into an elegant book.

Abbreviations and Short Titles

AN — Anglo-Norman

Awntyrs — *The Awntyrs off Arthure at the Terne Wathelyn*, ed. Ralph Hanna (Manchester, 1974)

DOST — *A Dictionary of the Older Scottish Tongue...*, ed. William A. Craigie, A. J. Aitken, *et al.*, 12 vols (Chicago, Aberdeen, and Oxford, 1937–2002). Online at the *DSL*

DSL — *Dictionary of the Scottish Language*, www.dsl.ac.uk

Duff — E. Gordon Duff, rev. Lotte Hellinga, *Printing in England in the Fifteenth Century: E. Gordon Duff's bibliography, with supplementary descriptions, chronologies and a census of copies* (London, 2009)

EETS — The Early English Text Society
- e.s — extra series
- o.s. — original series
- s.s. — supplementary series

Gawain — *Sir Gawain and the Green Knight*, ed. J. R. R. Tolkien and E. V. Gordon, rev. Norman Davis (Oxford, 1967)

Golagros — *The Knightly Tale of Golagros and Gawane*, ed. Ralph Hanna from materials collected by the late W. R. J. Barron, STS 5th ser. 7 (Edinburgh, 2008)

Howlat — *Richard Holland, The Buke of the Howlat*, ed. Ralph Hanna, STS 5th ser. 12 (Edinburgh, 2014)

IMEV — Carleton Brown and Rossell H. Robbins, *Index of Middle English Verse* (New York, 1943), with Robbins and John L. Cutler, *Supplement to IMEV* (Lexington, KY, 1966)

L — Robert Lekpreuik's 1572 print of *Rauf*

ME — Middle English

MED — *The Middle English Dictionary*, https://quod.lib.umich.edu/m/med

NLS — The National Library of Scotland, Edinburgh

OE — Old English

OED — *The Oxford English Dictionary*, www.oed.com/

OF — Old French

ON — Old Norse

OSc — Older Scots

Riddy	*Rauf Coilyear*, ed. Felicity Riddy in *Longer Scottish Poems Volume One, 1375–1650*, eds Priscilla Bawcutt and F. Riddy (Edinburgh, 1987)
RSTC	*A Short-Title Catalogue of Books Printed in England, Scotland and Ireland and of English books printed abroad 1475–1640*, ed. A. W. Pollard *et al.*, 2nd edn, 3 vols (London, 1976–91)
SND	*The Scottish National Dictionary* (as *DOST*)
STS	The Scottish Text Society
Whiting	Bartlett J. Whiting, *Proverbs, Sentences and Proverbial Phrases from English Writings Mainly Before 1500* (Cambridge, MA, 1968)

Introduction

The 1572 print and Robert Lekpreuik

We know *The Taill of Rauf Coilȝear* on the basis of a single surviving witness to a 1572 printed edition (*RSTC* 5487), now preserved as NLS H.29.c.9. This volume, available in full facsimile (*Taill*, ed. Beattie 1966), may be described as:

Title-page: [a row of hedera] ¶ Heir beginnis the taill | of Rauf coilȝear how | he harbreit King | charlis [woodcut] [rosette] Imprentit at Sanc- | tandrois be Robert Lekpreuik. Anno. 1572.

Contents: sig. [A i] title-page, with blank verso; sigs A ij^{r}–[D iv^{r}] the text of the poem (IMEV 1541); sig [D iv^{r}] [a further woodcut, discussed below, p. 5 n.7]; sig [D iv^{v}] blank.

Collation: 4°: A–D^{4} (signed A ii, B i–iii, C i–iii, D i–ii).

Binding: early s. xix, gold-tooled russet morocco (Beattie 1966:vii).

The descent of this book remains obscure for nearly two centuries. It appeared, as part of a *Sammelband*, in an Edinburgh auction in 1736, where it was purchased by the Advocates' Library (Beattie 1966: vii–iii). In addition to the print version of *Rauf Coilȝear*, this composite volume included six further separate productions, all of them printed by Wynkyn deWorde, *c.* 1500, and with a strongly devotional slant. These are now:

NLS H.32.b.15 = Duff 398, *RSTC* 5573: *The moost excellent treatise of the thre kynges of Coleyne*, 4° in 8s, Wynkyn deWorde's second edition (of four), after July 1499.

NLS H.32.b.20 = Duff 2, *RSTC* 13610: *The abbaye of the holy Ghost*, 4°, deWorde's third edition (of three), [1500?].

NLS H.32.b.21 = Duff 372, *RSTC* 22597: [John Skelton] *Here begynneth a lytell treatyse named the bowge of courte*, 4° in 6s, deWorde's first edition (of two), [1499?].

NLS H.32.b.22 = Duff 13, *RSTC* 279 [John Alcock, bishop of Ely] *Mons perfeccionis...*, 4° in 6s, deWorde's second edition (of four), 23 May 1497.

NLS H.32.b.23 = Duff 225, *RSTC* 14081: *Informcion for pylgrymes vnto the holy londe*, 4°, deWorde's first edition (of three, though no printer ascribed in the book), [1500?].
NLS H.32.b.24 = Duff 272, *RSTC* 17033 [John Lydgate] *Here begynneth ye temple of glas*, 4° in 8s, deWorde's first edition (of three, though again no printer is ascribed in the book), [1500?].

The Advocates' curators' records suggest these were bound in the order: *Information – Kings – Abbey – Bowge – Temple – Rauf*. They do not mention Alcock's *Mons perfeccionis*, a fact that suggests it might have been a separate lot or from another sale and joined later with similar productions. The relative homogeneity of the remainder, as well as the concluding position of *Rauf*, certainly implies that this had originally been a collection assembled in London *c.* 1500, with *Rauf* a late intrusion. The current binding must postdate 1821, when the poem was discovered, 'bound at the rear of other materials', presumably the now disaggregated *Sammelband*; the discovery produced the *editio princeps*, Laing's quasi-facsimile edition (1822, 1826).[1] Unlike the similar Chepman and Myllar prints, none of these pamphlet-like productions has information added in early hands that would indicate provenance (only inscriptions affixed by Advocates' librarians).

Although a number of references indicate that the poem, or at least some comparable 'taill' concerning Rauf Coilȝear, was well-known from an early date (see below, 'Language and Date'), only a single reference to another copy survives. 'Þe buke of ralf colȝear' appears in the contemporary contents-list for a now-lost portion of the Asloan manuscript (NLS, MS 16500, formerly Acc. 4233, *c.* 1513 x 1530), where it followed another Scots stanzaic alliterative poem, *Golagros and Gawane* (see Craigie 1923–25:1, xv). *Golagros* had appeared in a surviving 1508 production of Scotland's first printers, Chepman and Myllar, and one suspects that Asloan transcribed *Golagros*, as he did several other of their texts, from the printed edition. One might, on this indirect evidence, infer that Lekpreuik's 1572 edition was not completely *de novo*, but a resetting from an earlier print.

1 I am grateful to the NLS conservator Simone Cenci for further information obtained during recent work on the binding. Lekpreuik's *Rauf* shows prickings from an earlier oversewing in a different binding. However, in the absence of similar inspection of the other separately bound portions of the original, it remains unclear whether these reflect the combined volume or a separate binding unique to *Rauf*.

Robert Lekpreuik had a contentious, if broken, printing career spanning two decades.[2] (He may have been imprisoned for his activities for nearly all his last seven years.) In spite of Mann's efforts at offering a normalising extenuation of his activities (e.g., 2000:150–51), he was clearly – and perhaps particularly at the time he took up *Rauf Coilȝear* – a distinctly, and often virulently, Protestant printer. His patronisation by the incipient Kirk is perhaps most evident in his 1567 appointment for twenty years as King's Printer with a monopoly for the production of many basic books, for example:

> Donatus pro pueris, Rudimentis of Pelisso, The actis of parliamentis, The croniklis of this realme, The buik callit Regia Majestas, The psalmes of David with the inglis and latine catechismes les and mair, The buik callit the Omelyis for reidaris in kirkis, Togidder with the grammer to be set furth callit the generall grammer to be usit within scolis of this realme for the eruditioun of the youth.[3]

This grant was quickly followed by a further licence, for a task Lekpreuik never took up, to print an 'Inglis Bibill' (i.e., Calvin's Geneva version, with its contentious theological marginalia). These privileges, importantly, were extended by the Protestant king during the 'civil war' with his orthodox mother. As Watry's important study points out (1993:4), the strong emphasis upon schoolbooks (Donatus, Pelisso, 'the generall grammer') bespeaks Protestant suspicion of continental education, perceived as undoubtedly tinged with papistry, and efforts to ensure an appropriate local form of basic instruction.

Moreover, the production of *Rauf Coilȝear* came at a point when Lekpreuik's Protestant affiliations had driven him from Edinburgh.[4] He had already, in 1570, been forced to accept civic licensing for any printing he undertook; after local government passed to 'the Queen's

2 Dickson-Edmond's extensive account (1890:198–272) has provided the basis for all subsequent discussions. See also Aldis 1970: nos 82–83, 98, 113. In addition there are entries for both Charteris and Lekpreuik in the Oxford *Dictionary of National Biography*. MacDonald (1998:92–95), in emphasising the huge investment in Protestant texts and their printing, debunks the influence of Henry Charteris's efforts in the 1590s, but ignores his earlier relations with printers like Lekpreuik on distinctly Scottish projects. Bawcutt's account (1998:64–65) may be somewhat more balanced.

3 The citation is from Dickson-Edmond (1890:201).

4 Summarising Dickson-Edmond (1890:202–5); they describe the books Lekpreuik produced at this time at 248–61 (and cf. 240–41).

party' in April 1571, and he was threatened with confiscation and imprisonment, Lekpreuik went into an eighteen-month internal exile. He was first at Stirling, the site of James's court, and subsequently at the Protestant hotbed, St Andrews, where *Rauf* was printed – and John Knox at the time resident. (I would note parenthetically that Lekpreuik's subsequent return to the capital was scarcely triumphant; he was jailed, perhaps for as long as seven years, and lost his equipment for the unlicensed printing of yet another controversial Protestant tract.)

But amidst these partisan travails, like all printers, Lekpreuik undertook 'odd-job' work that would keep his press in operation and the cash flowing. His *Rauf* probably, but not certainly, represents the last endeavour in a brief, yet apparently productive partnership with Scotland's greatest late sixteenth-century bookman, Henry Charteris. This extended Charteris's earlier activities in promulgating Scots literary texts (at this time he was but a book-seller, only branching into printing in the 1580s).[5]

Charteris began this endeavour with a particularly ambitious project, a complete works of the popular Stewart court poet Sir David Lindsay (*d.* 1555). This, given already extensive printings of Lindsay, including by Charteris's partner the printer John Scot, would run to two volumes, which appeared in 1568 and 1571 (*RSTC* 15658 and 15659). More or less simultaneously, probably inspired by the success of the first Lindsay volume (since he would not have proceeded, had it not been a lucrative proposition), Charteris engaged Lekpreuik to produce prints of further, in this case early, Scots texts. Two of these productions, cheap unadorned editions of Henryson's *Moral Fables* (*RSTC* 185) and of Hary's *Wallace* (*RSTC* 13149) appeared in Edinburgh in 1570. Like *Rauf*, they are in (antiquity-signalling) black-letter, not Lekpreuik's usual type-font, and both, like the earlier Lindsays, announce that they were produced 'at the Expensis of Henrie Charteris: and ar to be sauld in his Buith, on the North syde of þe gait, abone the Throne' (i.e., in Edinburgh's High Street, west of the 'Weigh-house') A further edition, that of Barbour's *Bruce* (*RSTC* 1377.5), followed, probably in 1571.

Although Lekpreuik was shortly to flee the capital, his relations with Charteris did not cease, and indeed became more varied. The first evidence for this continuing connection is provided by two publications from the printer's initial exile in Stirling, the site of 'the King's court'. He produced there two editions of the king's tutor George Buchanan's

5 For this episode (and the information adduced below), see Wattry (1993:24–41).

Ane admonition direct to the trew Lordis, a text in defence of James against evil counsellors (*RSTC* 3966.5 and 3968).

While given Lekpreuik's unabashed courting of controversy, these publications do not surprise, they had consequences that must have involved Charteris as well. Not only was Lekpreuik's Buchanan reprinted at Stirling, but in London as well, by another reformist printer, John Day.[6] Indeed the title-page of Day's version (*RSTC* 3967) proclaims its origins, 'accordyng to the Scotish copie Printed at Striuilyng by Robert Lekpreuik'. This transaction clearly involved Charteris, because whatever the financial dealings underlying the London reprinting, it also involved an 'in-kind' payment as well. Day had previously used (in *RSTC* 14075) a woodcut image of an elderly couple in conversation; this reappears almost immediately as a decorative feature in Charteris's second volume of Lindsay's works (not Lekpreuik's product), and again, probably in the same year, in Lekpreuik's *Bruce*. This book was, of course, produced under Charteris's auspices. Moreover, Lekpreuik retained the woodcut, and it appears, perhaps a little incongruously (as simple space-filler?), on the title page of the St Andrews publication of concern here, *Rauf Coilȝear* (see the frontispiece to this volume).[7] This production, again, shows the black-letter of Lekpreuik's earlier adventures with Older Scots, but only this implicit connection with projects undertaken for Charteris.

Language and Date

My earlier editions of alliterative materials provide extensive accounts of their northern and Scots dialectal features (see *Golagros* xxiv–xxxi, *Howlat* 16–23). The rhyming evidence for these forms is nearly completely reproduced in the transmitted text of *Rauf Coilȝear*.[8] Conse-

6 Day was, for example, in 1567–68 the preferred outlet for texts associated with Elizabeth's archbishop Matthew Parker, the first printer to use the Anglo-Saxon typefont developed for Parker's secretary John Joscelyn. See further Lucas 1997.

7 The second illustration of Lekpreuik's *Rauf* is apparently unique. Dickson-Edmund describe this as 'a rude woodcut of a king standing by an open window, pointing with a sceptre to a person walking away from him' (1890:255), just plausibly, given the rather stylish late Stewart outfits (although not the knight's harness the poem describes), an image not involving Rauf, but Charlemagne saluting Roland as he leaves court. For a different view, see Beattie's suggestion (1974, 115) that it is a reused Psalter woodcut showing David sending Uriah off to war (and death).

8 Down to such a minor feature as regular Scots *mocht* 'might', in rhyme here at 268, 384, 490, and 914; cf. *Golagros* xxx n.36.

quently, I provide here an abbreviated account devoted to a few telling features distinctively Scots, items 13–16 in the account provided at *Golagros* (again, dependent on the definitive Aitken 2002).

Point 13: In early Scots, earlier long *a* coalesces at an early date with the diphthong /ai/, a development ubiquitously attested in *Rauf*:

1 *chiftane* (OF *-aine*, but in an unstressed syllable):3 *ane* (OE *ān*), etc.
48 *trauale* (OF *travail*):52 *hale* (OE *hāl*)
243 *saill* (OE/ON *sala*):244 *trauaill*, etc.[9]

Point 14: From the mid-fifteenth century, this earlier *ā/ai* (presumed originally to be *ā*) coalesces with earlier Scots long *e* as *ē*. Recognising the development is often difficult (and has proved confusing to editors). Yet it is well attested in *Rauf*, even in the absence of rhyme, because sporadically hidden under various back-spellings. Clear rhyming examples include:

28 *baid* (OE *bād*);30 *raid* (OE *rād*):32 *straid* (OE *strād*):34 braid (OE *brǣdu*) [cf. *breid* 593]
137 *laid* (for *led*, OE *lædde*):141 *graid* (ON *greidd*)
494 *haue* (ME *haven*):496 *craue* (OE *crafian*):498 *gaif* (for *geif*, ON *gefa*):500 *saue* (AN *sa(u)ver*) [cf. *geif* 610]
592 *weid* (OE *wǣd*):593 *on breid* (OE *brād*);594 *ȝeid* (OE *ēode*)

Three of these examples rhyme historic *ā* and *ē*, the second historic *ai* and *ē*. One prominent analogue for the development is the back-spelling *gaist* 'guest' (96, 104, and 108); but *gest* appears unproblematically in rhyme at 201 and 782.

To these instances, one should probably add:

216 *chier* (AN *che(i)r)*:217 *coilȝear* (OF *-ier*, but routinely rhyming elsewhere as if *-iar*):218 *feir* 'company' (OE *gefēra*)
455 *grene* (OF *greine*, *graine*):457 *tene* (OE *tēona*):459 *schene* (OE *scēne*):461 *sene* (ME *sēn[e]*)
662 *sene*:664 *betwene* (OE *betwēonan*):666 *grene* (as the prec.):668 *fyftene* (OE *fīftēne*)

9 This development is incipient, but only so, in northern ME, e.g., potentially *Awntyrs* 432 with *laith* (OE *lāþ*) rhyming with *feith* (OF *feid, feit*), etc.

The first again rhymes historic *ā* and *ē*, the latter two (involving the same word) historic *ai* and *ē*.

Point 15: OF *gn* rhymed with Scots *-ng*:
424 *letting* (OE *-ung*):425 king (OE *cyning*):426 *ling* 'line' (OF *ligne*).

I choose to interpret an earlier ambiguous example (395) otherwise, just as I would offer different explanations of some further anomalous instances, e.g., 60 *fechtine* and 896 *counsings* (the form recurs within the line at 913); see below, p. 9 and n.13.

Point 16: In Scottish alliterative practice, *v* and *w* regularly rhyme:
208 With **w**yne at thair **w**ill   and eik **v**ennysoun
886 For that **w**ar na **w**assalage,   sum men **w**ald say

The second of these points, number 14, proves especially significant, since it allows a relatively narrow dating of the poem. In his study of the Older Scots vowel system, Aitken finds the merger of *ā/ai* with *ē* alien to the usage of poets born in the earlier fifteenth century like Holland and Hary. In contrast, the merger is regular in poets born around and after 1460, like Dunbar.[10] If 1460 provides a *terminus a quo*, one can hardly expect the poem to represent a composition of much before 1485. Although Tonndorf's suggestion (*Taill* 1894:13–15) – that the poem's reference to the inheritance of Anjou (927) would date composition shortly after 1480 – was properly refuted as historically inaccurate as early as Browne's edition (*Taill* 1903:30–31), it is accidentally just about right.

Perhaps further evidence for such a dating in the 1480s emerges, ironically enough, from an argument thoroughly misbegotten. In his edition of the *Wallace*, Matthew P. McDiarmid argued at length for Hary's authorship of both *Golagros* and *Rauf* (1968–69:1, cviii–xxvii). In his effort to demonstrate the connection, he adduced a lengthy list of verbal parallels (cvii–xxi, and cf. parallels with *Howlat* in cxxiv n.1). While the cogency of these examples as indicating common authorship may be questioned, they do imply reliance on a common set of poetic stocks available around and just after the conclusion of Hary's work (in McDiarmid's account, 1478).

Thus, the poem is surely contemporary with *Golagros*, with which it shares a number of topics, perhaps features that led Asloan, who may

10 For fuller discussion, see *Golagros* xxix–xxx (and particularly nn.30–31).

have taken both texts from Chepman and Myllar prints, to copy the texts as if companion poems. Moreover, there is a particularly narrow window for composition, perhaps only ten to fifteen years, *c.* 1485–1501. References to a 'Rauf Coilȝear' (although not necessarily *Rauf* itself?) appear in poems written just at the turn of the sixteenth century, the first example securely dated 1501:

> I saw Raf Coilȝear with his thrawin brow,
> Craibit Iohne the Reif and auld Cowkewyis sow,
> And how the Wran come out of Ailssay,
> And Piers Plewman that maid his workmen fow...
> (Gavin Douglas, 'The Palice of Honour' 1711–14)

and:

> Quhone servit is all uther man,
> Gentill and sempill, of everie clan –
> Kyne of Rauf Colȝard and Iohnne the reif...
> (Dunbar, 'To the King' ['Schir, ȝit remember...'] 31–33)

In their immediate collocations, both poets recall a Rauf Coilȝear as exemplifying a rough, lower-class, and perhaps explicitly comic tradition. (Both also indicate that, like *Golagros*, the poem could well have been available to Chepman and Myllar for printing in 1508.) A later reference, in the mid-century *Complaynt of Scotland*, places the poem very differently, implicitly among noble romance topics. Yet this equally indicates the poem's continuing mid-century popularity (certainly a strong motivation for Lekpreuik's – and perhaps Charteris's – decision to print it).[11]

This is an adequate linguistic demonstration for editorial purposes. But any student of the poem will be aware of a range of more or less problematic rhymes. These, past editors customarily have queried as variously inexact. However, virtually without exception, all such examples fall into well-established classes of rhymes considered 'exact enough' in formal literary contexts down to at least Shakespeare (and

11 Cf. Wedderburn 1979:50: 'the tail of syr euan arthuris knycht, rauf collȝear, the seige of millan, gauen and gollogras, lancelot du lac, Arthour knycht...'. The listing is interestingly ecumenical, for the first text is apt to have been the northern ME *Ywain and Gawain*, and a second Charlemagne item, *The Siege of Milan*, intruding among a wave of Arthuriana, is also only known in northern ME (see n.19).

in informal contexts, to the present day). They are thoroughly unexceptionable, if not to overly formal modern taste.

One persistent licence concerns what one might identify as 'assonant rhyme'. That is, in the presence of the same vowel, exact phonetic correspondence between final consonants may be perceived as optional. Rhymes of this sort, recorded in profusion so early as Laȝamon, typically involve a specific phonetic context; 'cross-rhymes' usually occur only between unvoiced stops preceded by the same vowel. On this basis, 81 *meit* rhyming with words in *-eip* is unexceptional, as is 604 'begeck' rhyming as if it had the form the compositors set, *beget*.[12] A more distant analogy, which typically attracts no attention because endemic in Scots verse, concerns the dental stops /d/ and /t/. These, in keeping with widespread phonetic variation in Scots, rhyme irrespective of voice (perhaps a reflection of sporadic final devoicing). Compare persistent examples of 'warrant' spelled and rhyming in /d/ (122, 159, 586), or *send* 'sent' rhyming /d/ (251); and within the line *went* for 'wende' (690).

A second licence, also widespread and ancient, involves assonance in the presence of final nasals, viz. /n/, /m/, and /(n)ŋ/. All these routinely rhyme with one another (and with one another in 'homorganic' clusters like /nd/:/ng/). Thus there is nothing exceptional about such forms as 162 *blame* (:*tan*, etc.), 311 *name* (:*lane*, etc.), or 674 *deme* (:*sene*, etc.). Two examples mentioned under point 15 above, at 60 and 896, probably also reflect this practice, with rhymes of /n:(n)ŋ/ (in this instance re-enforced by such commonplace forms as *nuffin*, which show regular reduction of *-nŋ*).[13]

The one apparently exceptional difficulty in rhyme concerns 766 *ken* (:*man*, etc.). However, this apparent exception can be resolved. Since the Older Scots verb *can* does not represent simply a bland auxiliary ('to be able to'), but has lexical force, as witnessed in *DOST*, where its

[12] Rhymes of this type still regularly appear in popular music, perhaps especially among singers with southern American backgrounds, e.g., 'If the river was whisky, I would be a diving *duck*; | Dive down to the bottom and, lord, I'd never come *up*', or 'Found dead people in the forest, | Tallahatchie river and *lakes*; | The whole world is wondering | What's wrong with the United *States*'.

[13] One should note that Lekpreuik's compositors had similarly reduced forms, as evidenced in their back-spellings *cunnings* 207, *courtingis* 265, and *cussingis* 913. Acknowledging this licence highlights some aspects of the poet's friskiness, for example the essentially monorhymed stanza at 233ff. (*-ame*:*-ane*) (as well as the 'near-miss' example at 350ff., *-is*:*-ayis*). Cf. the textual note to 132.

semantic field overlaps with that for Older Scots *ken* ('to know'), the forms would therefore have had a tendency to merge, especially given their consonance.

Although these rhymes reveal a poem written in traditional Older Scots, the compositors' practice shows a good many passing examples of either 'anglicisation' or 'modernisation'. Twice the traditional present participle in *-and* is otherwise reproduced: 347 *following*, 397 *cumming*. Scots *ill* is preserved, where it is necessary for rhyme (39, 54, 108), but otherwise universally presented as *euill* (on one occasion, line 743, clearly erroneously). On three occasions (647, 661, 724), the plural *this* appears where one would expect *thir* (contrast 689). Compositorial practice has confusingly reduced the distinction between the negative particle *not* and the emphatic noun *nocht*. One typeset form, 765 *wythest* (representing *wychtest*), a century earlier might have been taken for a distinctly East Anglian English form.[14]

Sources

Speaking generally (although I offer a qualification at p. 11 below), the issue of the poet's sources had been resolved before Amours's foundational edition of 1892–97. The greater portion of the poem (roughly lines 1–776) has been derived from a common English ballad narrative, typically called 'the king in disguise'. In such accounts, a king, unrecognisable as such in his travelling clothes, is forced to take rude shelter; in most accounts, following upon a shocking revelation of his identity (and social centrality), he munificently repays his 'busteous' and shocked host for hospitality received.[15]

To this longstanding and common narrative, *Rauf Coilȝear*, unique in insular examples in identifying the king as Charlemagne, adds a specifically 'romance' episode. This draws upon the traditional associations of the Frankish king as warrior against the Moors and Islam. Here Rauf, newly promoted to knighthood as reward for his *herbergage*, inadvert-

14 Past editorial silence about the rhymes at 797 and 874 (*hecht* and *fecht* rhyming *hicht* and *ficht*) adequately indicates that these are not analogous examples. Cf. for example, *Golagros* 520, *Howlat* 486. On the general topic, see further Aitken 1997.

15 The outstanding discussion is Child 2003 [originally 1898]:5, 67–87; this builds upon materials assembled at Herrtage 1882:v–vi. With marginal exceptions, discussed below, Smyser 1932 largely reprises Child's materials (e.g., 138–39 n.4).

ently faces a heathen knight (see further the textual note to line 803). Through the arrival of Charlemagne's paladin Roland, the scene is transformed, as in other Charlemagne materials, from a pitched battle to a pitch for conversion. The 'Saracen', won over by Roland's blandishments, rather speedily converts to Christianity, and the poem concludes with a crescendo of endings pleasant for all.

A quite substantial group of examples of 'the king in disguise' survives in ME. Among these are IMEV 988 (*The King and the Shepherd*), 989 (*John the Reeve*), 1769 (*The King and the Hermit*, reprised in Scott's *Ivanhoe*), and 4168 (*The King and the Barker*). To this already extensive collection, Child's ballad 273 adds the early modern examples *King Edward the Fourth and a Tanner of Tamworth* and *The King and the Miller of Mansfield*.[16]

Since Hazlitt's 1895 reprinting of Laing's *editio princeps* of *Rauf Coilȝear*, but a single of these texts has featured prominently as a direct inspiration for this poem. Although it now survives only in a seventeenth-century transcription, the Percy Folio Manuscript (British Library, MS Additional 27879), *John the Reeve*, a bit hopefully dated as pre-1461, shows closer affinities to the poem than any other known version. Smyser (1932:138–45) offers a detailed and protracted argument for *John the Reeve* as the exact source used by the Scots poet. For Smyser, the main resemblance between the two texts, which he finds only attenuated elsewhere, concerns 'the description of the luxurious domestic life of the "humbler subject"' (138).

Perhaps the closest 'literary' analogue, certainly a poem that has provoked a variety of critical dialogue relevant to *Rauf*, is *Sir Gawain and the Carl of Carlisle* (IMEV 1888). This lacks the predominant motif of 'the king in disguise', but certainly offers ample analogies between 'the carl' and Rauf as roughly courteous hosts. As the title indicates, *The Carl* is a poem with a northwestern setting, and one might notice that, at least nominally, this is shared with *John the Reeve*, which includes a few, rather vague Lancashire references. (Percy did not find his manuscript in the northwest at all, but the property of a Shropshire landowner.) Such provenances might well testify to exchange, seepage, or simply common interests in the English West March and adjacent Borders, a feature shared with *Awntyrs*, a poem written in the thirteen-line stanza also used for *Rauf*.

In contrast to possibly exact derivation from *John the Reeve*, *Rauf*'s connection with earlier Charlemagne materials might be

[16] For a recent edition of the first three of these, see Furrow 2013.

construed as somewhat attenuated. Certainly, generically similar (and one might observe, predictably general) situations are integral to the Charlemagne cycle. These begin with the purportedly foundational 'historical' account, *The pseudo-Turpin Chronicle*, a narrative of Charlemagne's Spanish adventurism alleged to be an eye-witness narrative penned by the conqueror's archbishop Turpin. (He appears in *Rauf* at 343.) Here the encounter between Roland and Vernagu (the Arabic name 'Farragut') proves tragic. In spite of Roland's protracted appeals for the spiritual benefits of Christian belief, the Muslim warrior will *not* convert; a mighty champion dies of his battle wounds unbaptised and unshriven.[17]

More directly analogous to the narrative in *Rauf* are two Middle English romance versions of this material. These appear in the London 'Auchinleck Manuscript' (NLS, MS Advocates' 19.2.1) of the 1330s. Both extensive fragments, these are *Roland and Vernagu* and *Otuel, a knight* (IMEV 823.3, 1103 [cf. IMEV 1996]).[18] These analogues are indeed closer to the poem; in them, Vernagu is explicitly a messenger (as is *Rauf*'s Magog), and in both, Roland's appeals for conversion are successful and convince the initially recalcitrant Muslim. Yet as analogues, these are relatively distant. Although the poet of *Rauf* was certainly well aware of Charlemagne romance (and of its grosser conventions), there is very little directly borrowed matter. Although Smyser was expert in this tradition, he discovered but a single verbal link between *Rauf* and any of the relevant materials (148). *Rauf*'s lines 343–44 form a plausible reminiscence of the French *Fierabras*, lines 6192–93:

> The gentill bischop Turpine   cummand thay se
> With threttie conuent of preistis   reuest at ane sicht

> Cel jour ot x. evesques ensembles revestis,
> Si ot arcevesques et abes xxxvi.[19]

[17] Herrtage 1882:xvii–xxiii prints the Latin *pseudo-Turpin*'s account of the encounter; for a fifteenth-century English version, see *Turpines Story* 2004:23/715–29/934.

[18] Both appear in Herrtage 1882, *Roland and Vernagu* at 35–61, *Otuel* at 63–116.

[19] But cf. McDiarmid 1968–69:1, cxxv n.4, who connects the detail with the northern ME *Siege of Milan* (see n.11).

At the same time, as Smyser himself admits (esp. 1932:147 n.2), the poet here shows considerable independence in responding to the tradition. Smyser calls attention to the chastened Roland figure, who never fights without Charles's consent (see 392) and who is uncharacteristically forbearing in his meeting with Rauf. One might also notice the slightly salacious moment at 532–33, Roland's self-presentation as amorous courtly dandy. This comment certainly strikes a note decidedly opposed, for example, to the hero's presentation in the *Chanson de Roland*; there the fact that Roland has a wife (who expires on news of his death) seems a distinct after-thought in the context of suicidally *preux* militarism. However, such dandyism is thoroughly of a piece with Rauf's somewhat bemused response to Roland's armorial finery, his wonder whether there is in fact a capable warrior, rather than just a braggart, lurking inside all the stuff (cf. n.7 above).

Moreover, the climactic encounter with Magog is not Roland's at all. (See the note to line 883.) Indeed, in the poem he is allowed to exhibit no prowess (although Magog acknowledges that he has done so in the past), and in a reversal every reader recognises, any battle honours are Rauf's. Further, the appeal to which the 'Saracen' responds is, from our perspective at least, only perfunctorily religious. Roland offers a rather commonplace fifteenth-century view of intercessory prayer – that while it attends to the fate of those departed (the hope of a heavenly dwelling), it is equally and always offered for 'the good estate', the continued prosperity, of the living. In an echo of the title-figure's ennoblement, Magog responds to an appeal financial in nature, a wedding with an heiress.

Alliterative Verse and *Rauf Coilȝear*

Rauf is one of three fifteenth-century Scots alliterative poems written in stanzas. This form of binding traditional long-lines predicated upon initial rhyme into coherent units was developed in fourteenth-century England; it first appears in a poem copied at mid-century, 'Summer Sunday', and subsequently in *The Pistil of Swete Susan* (south Yorkshire, *c.* 1370) and *The Awntyrs off Arthure* (perhaps from Cumberland, *c.* 1400–20). Nothing except its completely English transmission would preclude the possibility that the latter poem was written in Scotland. Indeed, by *c.* 1420, Andrew Wyntoun refers to a poet 'Huchown of the Awle Ryale' as responsible for both *The Pistil of Suet Susane* and *the Awntyr of Gawane* (Wyntoun 1903–14: vol. 4, V.xiii.4311–12). While Wyntoun's ascription, which stimulated a huge and ultimately futile authorship controversy in the first decade of the twentieth century, is surely wrong in some detail, he offers testimony to early Scots knowledge of poems in this form.[20] And he is further prescient, since although this stanza-form may have been invented in England, its later development and popularity were predominantly Scots. The first surviving stanzaic poem certainly Scots is Richard Holland's *Buke of the Howlat*, from Morayshire in the late 1440s. Holland's poem was followed, about forty years later, by the two contemporary efforts, *Golagros and Gawane* and *Rauf*.

In his *Essayes of a Prentis*, James VI and I identifies this stanzaic form as 'rouncefallis or tumbling verse' (Craigie 1951–8, 1:81). Rather unusually for a stanza of mid-fourteenth-century origin without a refrain, 'rouncefallis' has an odd number of lines, thirteen in all. The first nine are, with certain optional modifications illustrated below, traditional alliterative long lines, but disposed within a rhyming pattern, ababababc. The odd-rhyming ninth line introduces a concluding 'wheel', four short lines of two or three stresses each; the first three of these rhyme together, and the last joins this conclusion to the ninth longline, viz. cdddc. Frequently in manuscript, as well as derived print renditions (including all the older Scottish prints), the concluding line is written to the right of the 'wheel' section opposite the eleventh line (Beattie 1966, v–vii); in some manuscript examples, the structure of part or all of the full stanzaic unit is clarified through rhyme-brackets. In early and prominent examples of the form, such as 'Summer Sunday', *The Three Dead Kings* or the first half of the *Awntyrs off Arthure*, the narrative frequently involves wilderness hunting scenes and a confrontation between proud and tyrannical worldlings and their ultimate limitation, the fact of death (Hanna in Holland 2014, 34 and note to line 976; Turville-Petre 1974).

As *Rauf*'s first stanza will indicate, the poet is well aware of the conventions of the form, including those adjustments to traditional practice that mark the stanzaic tradition. These I have previously described at length in *Golagros* (xxxix–xli). As on that occasion, I have marked the text to highlight the traditional alliterative features. Syllables bearing rhyme appear in bold-face, and I have highlighted b-verse syllabic patterns by marking stressed syllables 'C' and unstressed ones 'x'.

20 For the authorship controversy at its most flamboyant (and inconsequential), see for example Neilson (1903).

x C x x C
In the **cheif** tyme of **Char**lis, that **cho**sin **chif**tane,

x x x C x C
Thair **fell** ane **fer**lyfull **flan** within thay **fell**is wyde,

x C x x x C
Quhair **em**preouris and **er**lis and **vth**er mony **ane**

x x x C C
Turnit fra Sanct **Thom**as befoir the ȝule-**tyde**.

x C x x C
Thay **past** vnto **Par**is thay **proud**est in **pane**

x x x C x C
With mony **pre**latis and **prin**cis that was of mekle **pryde**.

x x C x C
All thay **went** with the king to his **wor**thy **wane**

x C x x C
Ouir the **feild**is sa **fair** thay **fure** be his syde.

x x C C
All the **worth**iest **went** **in** the morning...

These lines announce the poem's affinities from the start, and in a form distinctive in Scots stanzaic versions. For example, line 1 shows the hyperalliterated aa|aa (and rhymes on what is a difficult stave), as also do lines 3 and 5. Lines 4 and 6 display the tendency to associate alliterative and end-rhyme, and thus to violate the convention, universal outside stanzaic poetry, that the fourth stave of the line must not rhyme. Line 7 carries this technique yet further, that a line requires three alliterative rhymes, irrespective of position; and line 9, the tendency, particularly pronounced in Scots (and perhaps especially the contemporary *Golagras*) to use two rhyming sounds, not necessarily linking either the half-lines or metrically prominent syllables (here abb|[a]xx). Only lines 2 and 8 would pass muster outside this tradition. At the same time, the poet reproduces with exactitude the most basic requirement of the form, b- or off-verse syllabic constraints, the rule that this part of the line must include two intermediate dips, one of no or one syllable, the other of two or more.

Moreover, such traditional metrical presentation is matched at the level of alliterative diction. The opening line transposes the first one of the stanzaic predecessor poems *Awntyrs* and *Golagros* – 'In the tyme of Arthur an aunter bytydde', 'In the tyme of Arthur, as trew men me tald', respectively – into Frankish context. Both *Awntyrs*'s *tyde* and *Golagros*'s line 2 *turnit on a tyde* are repeated in the rhymes of the stanza, among further echoic details. And of course, the poet immediately introduces the same scene as do these poems, lordly men seeking succour in a sudden storm.[21]

The poem's opening continues in this mode. It is, within the parameters of stanzaic poetry, absolutely precise and fully alliterative for its first four stanzas. The form begins to crack only when Charles addresses the collier at line 53:

> 'Sa mot I thrife', said the king, 'I speir for nane ill...'

If there is alliterative marking here, it is misplaced; initial rhyme falls on words that throughout alliterative tradition (and not just the stanzaic) cannot bear it. Thus, the ostensible rhyme on /s/ is almost completely decoupled from stress (here presumably falling on *thrife-king-speir-ill*). Moreover, if *Sa* and *said* offer a rhyme, the line violates one of the hoariest rules of Germanic prosody (a reflection of underlying developments from Indo-European), that /s/ must rhyme apart from /sp/ (and /st/ and /sk/, and that they must all rhyme apart from one another). And generally speaking (contrast line 32), the poet will persist in ignoring this rule throughout the poem.

Indeed, much of the poem more closely resembles line 53 than it does the first four stanzas. Although the poet scrupulously follows the form of his inherited thirteen-line stanza and, even in the sloppy form in which *Rauf* has been transmitted, attends carefully to b-verse syllabic constraints, substantial portions are not written to alliterative pattern. Walsh's positivistic report (*Tale* 1989:42) of the alliterating patterns, while not exact, is representative – and revelatory.[22] In her account:

- 49 lines have the alliterative rhyme-form standard in ME verse aa|ax.
- Another 92 lines show the expected tendency (as is impermissible outside stanzaic contexts) to rhyme the fourth stave in a line with three rhyming words, i.e., the patterns aa|xa, xa|aa, and ax|aa.
- 84 lines represent the hyper-rhymed form aa|aa expected in the Scots stanzaic tradition.
- 18 lines have some form of double-alliteration, i.e., patterns like aa|bb, ab|ab, etc.

[21] Storm descriptions conventionally have been seen as one of the persistent rhetorical topics defining this tradition; see Shepherd 1970, Jacobs 1972, Turville-Petre 1977:105–6 and passim.

[22] The figures Walsh reports are not consistent, and appear to me to ignore more than 200 of the 675 relevant lines.

This is a total of around 240 lines one might take as representing 'normal alliterative usage'. Against this showing, Walsh reports 128 lines that show no alliteration at all. A further 105 lines in her account show fragmentary patterns generally seen as impermissible elsewhere in the tradition (and perhaps especially so in typically hyperrhymed stanzaic Scots examples), e.g., aa|xx, ax|ax, xa|ax, etc. Thus, nearly half the lines in Walsh's survey would not pass muster at all in a traditional alliterative poem.

Nor is this in *Rauf Coilȝear* simply a matter of metrical patterning. As any self-respecting poet faced with line 53, cited above, would see, the poem's diction and lexical use defy the normal conventions of the form. Even a challenged practitioner should see that line 53 might easily be a perfectly good alliterative line –

> 'Sa mot I **speid**', **spak** the king,   I **speir** for nane ill...' –

here apparently mangled with deliberation. The poem relies upon a number of very commonplace words, thus reflecting colloquialism, rather than any 'poetic diction'. A number of items on copious display, e.g., *king*, *knicht*, and *man*, quite clearly indicate the poet's avoidance of one feature basic to alliterative poetry, the substitution of alliterative rhyming synonyms for prosaic concepts. (Although such occur, e.g., *segge* and *grome*, they are remarkably thin on the ground.) My glossary is also marked by a very large number of phrasal entries, further testimony to the colloquial and conversational métier on offer here. Additionally, the textual notes draw attention to a heady number of rare lexical forms; these must reflect a vocabulary drawn from outwith alliterative, indeed any other written, diction.

Thus, Charles's refusal to speak alliteratively in line 53 seems to me a litmus moment in the poem. Another, probably more explicit one, since it draws direct attention to language, occurs a great deal later:

> Mekle merwell *of that word*   had Schir Rolland;
> He saw na wappinis thair (514–15, my emphasis).[23]

Roland looks to check out whether Rauf is bearing arms, but he is stimulated to do so by Rauf's language, his preceding speech. This, which I

23 Cf. the characterisation of 'Rauf-speak', here for other reasons, as a *raifand word* 649; but equally note how Magog will make a comparable charge against Roland at 894.

present in marked form, Roland, whose appearance has in previous lines been marked by persistent alliterative diction, finds startling;

x C x x x C
'Thow **fand** me sechand nathing   that **fol**lowit to **feid** –

x C x x C
I war ane **fule** gif I **fled**   and **fand** nane af**fray** –

x C x x C
Bot as ane **lauch**full man   my **laid**is to l**eid**,

x C x x C
That **leif**is with mekle **law**tie   and **lau**bour, in fay.

x C x x C
Be the **moth**er and the **mayd**in   that **maid** vs re**meid**,

C x x x x C
And thow **mar** me ony **mair**,   cum efter quhatsa **may**,

x C x x x C
Thow and I sall **dyn**tis **deill**   quhill ane of vs be **deid**

x x C C
For the **deid**is thow hes me **done**   vpon this **deir day.**' (506–13)

The underarmed Rauf, just a tradesman making his deliveries, has tended to address Roland in his usual demotic. But here he finds a heroic language, performs a perfect alliterative stanza, a traditional *bēot*. Moreover, this is marked not simply by adherence to all the verse rules, but by an additional feature of glitzy eloquence, each distych doubly marked by alliterative rhymes that continue across the pair of lines. Roland's wonder is well-placed: alliterative stock is here 'out of place' and yet simultaneously apt to the gruff and frequently belligerent, if unsuitably armed collier. At this moment, alliterative verse is simply not recognisable as apt by traditional, class-bound heroic characters.

Thus, I find the poem's métier revealing – and revealing of what every reader has always seen, the overturning here of the class-bounded chivalric ethos that seems inherent to the alliterative tradition. The note is struck almost immediately following Charlemagne's non-rhyming verse cited above. The king calls Rauf, either with quasi-paradoxical irony or in an at this point non-literal sense, *ane nobill fallow* (54). To this, Rauf responds by implicitly identifying the king as yet another *gude fallow... | Walkand wil of his way* (73–74), with its assumption that 'fellows' should be walking, not riding noble steeds.[24] Indeed, the poem

24 Similar jokes involving pronomial usage – addresses using polite *ye* or

might be seen as unique in concluding with a stanza that announces Rauf and his family's continuing integration into noble society – yet does so without any of the alliterative trappings that generally mark such an investiture (contrast *Awntyrs* 664–88). This is thus a poem about, *inter alia*, language contact and the integration of diverse modes of speech; it, carefully and with deliberation, provides a prosodic and stylistic analogue to its most overt thematic.

Thus, the poem stands as a kind of hybrid. While it very frequently declines the rhymed alliterative and its rhetoric, it nonetheless retains, fairly carefully, if sometimes ambiguously, the expected stress patterns and b-verse constraints of the received form. In doing so, it exposes the boundedness of alliterative tradition. In its customarily panegyric and decorative mode, such verse forms a tribute only to 'richesse' (and its presumed behavioural and moral accoutrements); here this is supplemented, if not overwhelmed, by a valued demotic. The absence of the rhyming synonyms for 'man', to take but a single example, is key here. Such lexis supports alliterative poetry as a pleonastic mode, one of repetition, given to parallel and variation, and one that manages to convey the same basic information multiply. The poem *Rauf* shows such ornamentation frequently undone by its hero's demotic directness.[25]

Here I would also draw attention to one feature of *Rauf Coilȝear*, its persistent attention to informal conversation, rather than public courtly address. One conventional marker of such an interest, provocatively signalled in Bradbury 2011, is the proverb, the conventional form of demotic wisdom.[26] To a degree no one has fully teased out, the poem is

(unduly? impolitely?) familiar *thou* – appear frequently; see the text notes to 89 and 158–59, and for royal *we*, 291.

25 Just a few further revelatory moments, driven by rhetorical context: Rauf's instructively broken example of the heroic, in a situation perhaps reminiscent of Gawain setting out to seek the Green Knight (377, 380–81); the poem's central stanza, the 38th (480–85), in which Rauf shows a capacity for responding to nobility and thinks to himself in 'thoroughly proper verse' (or its reprise at 661ff.); or the distinction between Roland's public blare in addressing his lord, succeeded by the non-alliterating language of private thought (585–604).

26 Although this reference to a recent study is here isolated, I have, in the absence of any similar tool, tried to construct an inclusive bibliography. A recent surge of interest in the poem has offered a range of provocative insights, particularly very interesting analogues with 'the monstrous host' in *Sir Gawain and the Carl of Carlisle*.

strewn with, and indeed driven by, examples, many highlighted in the textual notes.[27]

Thirteen-line poems, both English and Scots, are traditionally death-engaged, acts of *memento mori*. In this tradition, poets offer their frequently grisly images as chastisement of the overweening aristocrat, and *Rauf* is no exception, as its sporadic echoes of earlier efforts in this form demonstrate.[28] But rather than the overt images of mortality designed to terrorise aristocrats into moral behaviour – Rauf is no insubstantial spectre – this poet finds a way of instantiating such behaviour, linguistically and thematically.

Unlike flashy alliterative variation, proverbial discourse is traditionally associated with the demotic. It expresses Langlandian 'kind wit', common sense or natural wisdom. This language appeals to a very basic concept, customarily signalled by terms like *ressoun* or *skyll* or *suith*,[29] in the poem embodied in Rauf's ruder sense of linguistic and social proprieties. (For references to the abundant uses, see the glossary.) But 'ruling oneself by reason' is the lesson death-poetry is designed to teach, and the poet's investment in 'Rauf-speak' might be seen as a way of communicating to aristocrats – as it does, in the poem's depiction of their gradual acknowledgement of this language – an acceptable moral outlook.

The proverb is at least perceived as a form of folk wisdom, and thus, an evocation of a decorum consonant with the folk-tale background to much of the piece. But it is equally the case that the narrative of folk-tale includes or enacts proverbial injunctions. Probably the most pregnant example relevant to *Rauf* is the never cited, 'al day meeteth men at unset stevene'.[30] The poem's episodes, only dimly reflecting either of its most palpable sources, *John the Reeve* or *pseudo-Turpin* materials,

[27] Indeed, Amours (1897:xxxix) argues that the story exemplifies a French proverb 'Charbonnier est maître chez soi'. One might equally wonder whether the entire enterprise was stimulated by the equivalence implied in a simple pun *Charles/Carl:carll*.

[28] For further discussion, with additional references, see *Howlat* 33–34, 145–48 passim. Mapstone 1986 begins with this point, but generally considers explicit texts of advice (romance at 143–200). Extension of her arguments to consider a poem like *Rauf* remains a desideratum; cf. Kindrick 1984.

[29] The last term, of course, corresponds to Chaucerian *trouthe*, Langland's *truþe*, or Gawain's *trawþe*.

[30] 'People continually meet up on occasions they had not arranged', the form of Whiting M210; 1951, 95–96, s.v. Man 18, at Chaucer's 'Knight's Tale', *Canterbury Tales* I.1523.

have been constructed by playing this perception back on four occasions: Charlemagne lost and meeting Rauf, Rauf waylaid by Roland, Rauf meeting the 'fake Wymond' at court, and the joust-seeking Rauf running upon the unexpected Magog (with a subsidiary fifth instance, when Roland comes upon them both). This proverb, of course, is essentially the Boy Scouts' injunction, 'Be prepared [for anything]'. One might more trenchantly state the teaching as an injunction to self-control in any circumstance, even the most unforeseeable. Excepting the third iteration, overawed and embarrassed at court, Rauf proves in his way more capable than any of the characters at fulfilling the injunction.[31] With the collier's triumph, traditional poetic language is accommodated to his demotic.

This Edition and its Predecessors

The preceding ramble through alliterative minutiae is not out of place when one comes to consider the text of the poem. In my previous editions of works generically resembling *Rauf* (often to the considerable chagrin of STS's advisory readers, when I rejected what had been transmitted), I felt I could rely on what I knew of alliterative tradition and its usage in constructing a text. But here all bets are off, as it were; if anyone halfway conversant with the tradition could reconstruct Charles's line 53 as what it should be saying – and manifestly isn't – then alliterative know-how is clearly a danger in approaching the text.

One minor bit of conventional editorial practice, the handling of the already cited line 506, will illustrate the problem:

> Thow fand me sechand nathing   that followit to feid.

sechand is certainly what Lekpreuik's compositors set, the unambiguous reading. But several of the poem's editors (despite the fact that Rauf's insistence might suggest that *nathing* deserves a stress more prominent than *sechand*) have felt this an obvious error and the line clearly

31 I cite a large number of proverbial analogues in the textual notes, but here are a few extras: cf. 95 and 'Little kens the wife that sits by the fire how the wind blows cold' (Whiting 1949:192, s.v. Hot); or the general purport of the entire narrative to demonstrate Rauf 'firm as steill' (Whiting S698–712, cf. 1951:131, s.v. Steel); or the entire text's effort to offer a counter to *Howlat* and its death-lyric moral about over-reachers (Whiting W714, cf. 1951:163, s.v. Wretch).

intended to represent the emphatic rhyming pattern aa|aa. As a result, they read *fechand* 'bearing, bringing' to fulfil the pattern. But as the end of the stanza shows, Rauf is armed – if inadequately in Roland's perception, at least sufficiently to defend himself on the highway. Moreover, at the centre of this conversation is the issue of whether Rauf is engaged in something Roland would recognise as a legitimate search, pursuit, or (gasp!) quest. I'm afraid the *textus receptus* here is correct, and that the editors who have here emended have cast themselves in the image of Lekpreuik's compositors (and/or their ancestors in the transmission), too prone to attend to surrounding copy. Compare, for example, the compositorial mishap of similar inspiration, *tewellis* 474.

Further examples where editorial intervention might seem similarly attractive and should be resisted are not far to seek. Consider two relatively adjacent lines from later in the poem, Rauf's 636 and 640, respectively:

> For I haue oft-tymes swet   in seruice full sair

and

> Se that thow leis thame not,   bot ȝeme thame full ȝair.

Both examples are easy to correct, indeed almost automatically so. For the first, read *oft-syis* (like the preceding example, transformed into aa|aa), and for the second, begin the line *Luik* (unproblematic aa|bb). Yet it seems to me that the very transparency of such 'correction' might well be to the point. I'm inclined to read lines like these (and a fair number of others) as comic, jokes. They at least raise the interesting question as to whether Rauf is sometimes supposed to be seen as engaged in the 'near-miss alliterative'. In treating a servant with the contempt he thinks he is receiving (patronising noblesse vindicates Rauf's view of himself as hospitable host), is Rauf to be seen as 'talking up', attempting the voice of lordliness and getting it just a little wrong?

Thus, I have tried to keep a light hand and resist alliterative quick fixes. In the subsequent discussion (as well as the notes, where I discuss many problematic readings), I use the term 'the compositor(s)' to describe transmissional difficulties. This should be understood to include any and all of the agents of the poem's now-invisible underlying transmission. The text must originally have been set from manuscript. Given the very early references to *Rauf* as at least a well-known tale (p. 8 above), one might assume this manuscript to be the product of (for this period) relatively extensive circulation – and thus itself undoubtedly erroneous in some instances. A second layer of difficulty may have been intruded, were one to believe, as Asloan's lost copy may imply, that Chepman and Myllar printed the poem among their 1508 productions. As Craigie pointed out long ago (*The Actis* 1940), ample evidence (although I will qualify this shortly) indicates that Lekpreuik used the earlier printers' *Wallace* as setting copy for his 1570 edition. If that were the case for *Rauf* as well, Lekpreuik's team will have inherited at least two prior transmissional states.

Although the poem has been relatively seldom discussed until quite recently, it might well be described as 'much edited'. (For a full list of editions, see the Bibliography.) On the whole, the most perspicacious editors to have addressed the text were the learned ancients, Amours and Browne.

I find myself at variance with virtually all of my predecessors, who, far more frequently than their efforts at over-alliterising the text, seem to me to have been unduly accommodating to the *textus receptus*. Indeed, I find their absence of inquisitiveness sobering, since there appear to me a good many more problematic places in the text than have attracted past notice (e.g., the rhyme at 455 and 666), and I do not believe I have found them all. Moreover, protecting what Lekpreuik printed has involved past editors in a number of contorted textual explanations; few seem to have considered that, while *lectio difficilior* may be a guide to editorial practice, passages admitting (or alleged to be responding to) only last-gasp explanations might simply communicate erroneous readings. (This is a salient law of general editorial theory argued, at length and with bracing acerbity, in Housman's prefaces to his Juvenal and Lucan.) Perhaps most frequently, past editors have been over-narrowly focused on dealing with the poem's difficulties. Their attention has too frequently been engaged with parsing the single line, and they thus have resisted considering larger rhetorical structures.

The transmitted text includes a smallish number of manifest errors, corrected by all scholars. Here the keynote is the first use of *deip* in line 17, corrected from Laing's *editio princeps* on. The situation is instructive; at some point in the transmission, someone has been attracted to the use of *deip* as a stave later in the line, has anticipated it in copying or typesetting, and has inserted this echo for a correct reading. (Opinions as to what that might have been, of course, differ, a situation endemic in a *textus unicus*, where all alterations are hypothetical.)

Simultaneously, there is a fair number of instances, illustrating an opposite attentiveness to surrounding copy, dissimilation from neighbouring readings. A good many of these are inferential, for example in line 952 the transmitted, but defective off-verse, 'maid game and gle'. Here the appropriate disyllabic form, *gamin*, metrically required, has been lost in the repetitive sequence *-in an-*. I am certain a good many examples have escaped any detection (see the textual note to line 132 on the persistence of repetitions at all levels in the poem), and I would be reasonably certain that a number involves a rash of minor readings, a great many of them creating grammatical conundrums that have exercised past scholars.[32]

A few such demonstrable instances could scarcely be described as 'minor'. For example, on two occasions (Riddy at line 31, Putter at line 545), past scholars have provided compelling translations for rather opaque lines. While I describe these translations as 'compelling', I would acknowledge one limitation common to both: neither is an accurate translation of the line as transmitted. In both instances, following these suggestions requires emendation; suggestive translation points towards another form of attraction to copy, an echoic word necessary to the proffered meaning yet dropped from the transmitted text (examples of homeoarchy or homeoteleuthon). Riddy's example seems to me thoroughly clearcut, and I have emended; with Putter's, where matters are not so pellucid, I have, as in several instances elsewhere, restricted my comment in the relevant textual note to outlining a range of possibilities.

I have also made – and think the effort worth more protracted study than my immersion in two hundred lines from book 6 – some effort at assessing the behaviour of Lekpreuik's team by examining their text of Hary's *Wallace*.[33] Here, as I have indicated above, Craigie showed that Lekpreuik relied upon Chepman and Myllar's earlier print, not the unique manuscript of the poem (NLS, MS Advocates' 19.2.2). This is evident from the common inclusion of an extra stanza, the common subdivision of the text into chapters, and the agreement in a rash of minor variant readings, generally alien and inferior to the manuscript. At the same time, very sporadic instances in which Lekpreuik's text agrees with the manuscript (e.g., in including lines lost in the earlier

32 There is also quite a large number of often-repeated small otiose readings that one might suspect as originating in transmission, e.g., in 805 *with*[2] is otiose; persistent examples of *for to* and of *out of* (where *to* and *of* would have been sufficient), etc.

33 This effort is obviously qualified by the fact that, among many other conditions one might adduce, we have no idea whether Lekpreuik was accompanied into involuntary exile by his full production team.

print) indicate a complicating feature, that the 1570 printer may have had access to a second textual source.

I offer here the seven occasions in my brief sampling in which Lekpreuik's text disagrees with both older copies, manuscript and *c.* 1508 Chepman and Myllar print. On these occasions in *Wallace* book 6, Lekpreuik clearly innovated, and one might hope that the underlying motives for his errors would be suggestive in examining another of his texts, *Rauf*, the printshop's behaviour here not subject to so direct a scrutiny:

118 Quhill thar power my*cht* be in **harnes** boun] **armis** L
134 Quhy schir he said come ȝhe **no*cht* new our se**] **not ouir þe see** L
154 **Thi deme has beyne Iapit** or thow was born] **Thay dame was iapit** L
167 Than fra the stowmpe the blude out **spurgyt** [springit CM] **fast**] **sprang ful fast** L
169 In-to gret part it **m*er*ryt** off his sicht] **marrit him** L
232 P*ar*tyt thar me*n* **and** [syne CM] diu*er*s **gatis** [partis CM] yeid] **and**, **wayis** L
269 **Sa** [*om.* CM] he begane w*ith* strenth and stalwart hand] **Ay** L

(quoted from McDiarmid ed. 1968–9, although without his punctuation)

One tendency noteworthy across these examples is an attentiveness to metre, Hary's then innovative use of a fundamentally iambic decasyllable line. Repairs to apparently defective syllable counts (or misplaced stresses) account for the majority of the examples, certainly in 133, 167, and 269, probably 167 and 169.[34] While Hary's verse-form can scarcely be seen as analogous to the alliterative metre of *Rauf Coilȝear*, this behaviour has an analogue in Lekpreuik's generally fastidious reproduction of b-verses in the latter production (even if the required forms are cloaked by the spellings set). One might parenthetically note that such attentiveness probably led Lekpreuik to a second source for his *Wallace*, since fastidiousness over syllables will surely have been accompanied by a similar regard for rhymes destroyed by lines lost in the earlier print.

[34] While line 169 is a difficult fusion of two different constructions ('in[to] part'/'part of'), I think Lekpreuik misunderstood it; the prose restatement would run, 'it merryt into gret part of his sicht', and the supplied 'him' is otiose in the presence of 'his'.

The other evidence here offered is sparse, but it is at least consonant with behaviours I adduce repeatedly in the textual notes. Erroneous readings one might ascribe to attraction to surrounding copy (as I note above, frequently recognisable in *Rauf Coilȝear*), occur at least twice here. In 134, the compositor apparently dropped a syllable through homeoarchy ('*no*cht *ne*w') and had to patch the end of the line. In 154, the compositor set the properly plural 'Th*a*y' ('those') through anticipation of 'd*a*me h*a*s/w*a*s *ia*pit'. But he also assimilated the perfect to the simple past *was* later in the line, and as in the preceding example, the obvious metrical ballast to fill out the line, 'or *that* thou' has fallen victim to homeoarchy (*th*-...*th*-). On the other hand, 118 *armis* is simply a sloppy homeographic substitution (paralleled at *Rauf* 534 and perhaps elsewhere).

Yet it is equally the case that Lekpreuik did read Chepman and Myllar's print with a critical eye and made efforts to improve it. As a persistent practitioner of attraction to surrounding copy, he could recognise it in others. Thus, in 232, he identified the earlier printers' echoic error, '*Part*yt...*part*is', and correctly intuited what the text should be saying, even if he could not retrieve Hary's exact reading.[35] And while failing to recognise *springit* in 167 as a legitimate homeographic effort at a difficult word, he did see that it could not be a correct reading (*springan* is a strong verb) and took corrective steps. (Both these examples imply that Lekpreuik's reference to a second textual source was limited; he made no effort to use it as a constant check on Chepman and Myllar's readings.) On the whole, however brief, this little survey will, I hope, offer some support for the scepticism with which I sometimes view the 1572 version of *Rauf*.[36]

In these circumstances, I have determined to create a relatively conservative 'substantive text edition'. There seems to me ample evidence of the compositors setting for sense, without any necessary feeling for underlying form, e.g., rhymes that indicate pronunciations foreign to the spelling, unnoted examples of elision, the *gamin* I

35 One should notice that this form of 'amelioration' relies upon a response to surrounding context equally on offer in the printer's work, the dissimilation of repeated readings.

36 I offer one final note on the 1572 edition. This shows persistent alternation between spellings in *-lie*/*-ly* and *-rie*/*-ry*, variation that raises the possibility that the text was set in type by two hands. Although there are patches exclusively of one form or the other (and *-y*-types generally recessive), if there were two hands at work, they were not setting the book 'in forme'.

have already cited or *burneist* 662. I have not intruded to correct such misleading spelling forms, although all I would identify are indicated in the collations. These are otherwise devoted to positive emendations, which include *ill* for *euill* in 743, required by the metre and a substantive (these are different words), not just a spelling correction.

Editorial Procedure

My edition follows the spelling of Lekpreuik's print. However, I have intruded modern capitalisation and punctuation (much of the latter substantially revising that of my predecessors). I use the capital Ȝ 'yogh' for Lekpreuik's *Z*; the font for the lower-case letter, as customarily, represents both 'yogh' and 'z' and I have disambiguated it as appropriate – *z* appears only in *Sarazine*. I print þ for Lekpreuik's *y*-font when that is the clear intent. In addition to customary punctuation, I have presented the verse-lines with marked caesuras as a way of facilitating access, since the poem is outwith usual alliterative norms. In my transcription and collation, I have ignored turned type, e.g., *n* set for *u* or vice versa.

Heir beginnis the taill of Rauf Coilȝear, how he harbreit King Charlis

1.

In the cheif tyme of Charlis,   that chosin chiftane,   sig. A ii^r
Thair fell ane ferlyfull flan   within thay fellis wyde,
Quhair empreouris and erlis   and vther mony ane
Turnit fra Sanct Thomas   befoir the Ȝule-tyde.
Thay past vnto Paris   thay proudest in pane
With mony prelatis and princis   that was of mekle pryde.
All thay went with the king   to his worthy wane;
Ouir the feildis sa fair   thay fure be his syde.
All the worthiest went   in the morning,
Baith dukis and duchepeiris,
Barrounis and bacheleiris;
Mony stout man steiris
Of town with the king.

2.

And as that ryall raid   ouir the rude mure,
Him betyde ane tempest that tyme hard I tell:
The wind blew out of the eist   stiflie and s[t]ure;
The d[rift] durandlie draif   in mony deip dell.
Sa feirslie fra the firmament,   sa fellounlie it fure
Thair micht na folk hald na fute   on the heich fell.
In point thay war to parische   thay proudest men and pure;
In thay wickit wedderis   thair wist nane to dwell
Amang thay myrk montanis;   sa madlie thay mer.
Be it was pryme of the day
Sa wonder hard fure thay
That ilkane tuik ane seir way
And sperpellit full fer.

16   sture] slure L
17   drift] deip L

3.

Ithand wedderis of the eist   draif on sa fast
It all to-blaisterit and blew   that thairin baid.
Be thay disseuerit sindrie,   midmorne was past;
Thair wist na knicht of þe court   quhat way þe king raid.
He saw thair was na better [bute]   bot God at the last;
His steid aganis the storme   staluartlie straid.
He cachit fra the court –   sic was his awin cast –
Quhair nabody was him about   be fiue mylis braid.
In thay montanis, iwis,   [w]ox he all will   sig. [A ii^{v}]
In wickit wedderis and wicht
Amang thay montanis on hicht.
Be that it drew to the nicht
The king lykit ill.

4.

Euill lykand was the king   it nichtit him sa lait
And he na harberie had   for his behufe.
Sa come thair ane cant carll   chachand the gait
With ane capill and twa creillis   cuplit abufe.
The king carpit to the carll   withoutin debait,
'Schir, tell me thy richt name   for the rude lufe'.
He sayis, 'Men callis me Rauf Coilȝear,   as I weill wait;
I leid my life in this land   with mekle vnrufe,
Baith tyde and time   in all my trauale.
Hine ouir seuin mylis I dwell
And leidis coilis to sell.
Sen thow speiris, I the tell
All the suith hale'.

5.

'Sa mot I thrife', said the king,   'I speir for nane ill;
Thow semis ane nobill fallow,   thy answer is sa fyne'.
'Forsuith', said the coilȝear,   '+ taist quhen thow will,

31 bute] *om.* L
35 wox he] he wox L
54 thy] *for authorial* thyn
55 taist] traist L

For I trow and it be nocht swa,   sum part sal be thyne'.
'Mary! God forbid', said the king;   'that war bot lytill skill:
Baith myself and my hors   is reddy for to tyne.
I pray the bring me to sum rest,   the wedder is sa schill,
For I defend that we fall   in ony fechtine.
I had mekill mair nait   sum freindschip to find,
And gif thow can better than I,
For the name of Sanct Iuly,
Thow bring me to sum harbery
And leif me not behind'.

6.

'I wait na worthie harberie   heir neir [at] hand
For to serue sic ane man   as me think the –
Nane bot mine awin hous,   maist in this land,
Fer furth in the forest   amang the fellis hie. sig. [A iiir]
With-thy thow wald be payit   of sic as thow fand,
Forsuith, thow suld be welcum   to pas hame with me
Or ony vther gude fallow   that I heir fand,
Walkand will of his way,   as me think the,
For the wedderis ar [s]a fell   that fallis on the feild'.
The king was blyth quhair he raid
Of the grant that he had maid,
Sayand with hart glaid,
'Schir, God ȝow forȝeild'!

7.

'Na! thank me not ouir-airlie   for dreid that we threip,
For I haue seruit the ȝit   of lytill thing to ruse.
For nouther hes thow had of me   fyre, drink, nor meit,
Nor nane vther eismentis   for trauellouris behuse.
Bot micht we bring this harberie   this nicht weill to heip
That we micht with ressoun   baith thus excuse,
Tomorne on the morning,   quhen thow sall on leip,
Pryse at the parting   how that thow dois.
For first to lofe and syne to lak –   Peter! it is schame'.

66 neir at hand] neirhand L
74 sa] fa L

The king said, 'In gude fay,
Schir, it is suith that ȝe say'.
Into sic talk fell thay
Quhill thay war neir hame

8.

To the coilȝearis hous baith,   or thay wald blin;
The carll had cunning weill   quhair the gait lay.
'Vndo the dure beliue!   Dame, art thow in?
Quhy deuill makis thow na dule   for this euill day?
For my gaist and I baith   cheueris with the chin;
Sa fell ane wedder feld I neuer,   be my gude fay'.
The gude-wyfe glaid   with + gle to begin,
For durst scho neuer sit summoundis   that scho hard him say;
The carll was wantoun of word   and wox wonder wraith.
All abaisit for blame,
To the dure went our dame;
Scho said, 'Schir, ȝe ar welcome hame
And ȝour gaist baith'.

9.

'Dame, I haue deir coft   all this dayis hyre   sig. [A iii^{v}]
In wickit wedderis and weit   walkand full will.
Dame, kyith I am cummin hame   and kendill on ane fyre;
I trow our gaist be the gait   hes farne als ill.
Ane ryall rufe het fyre   war my desyre
To fair the better for his saik,   gif we micht win thairtill.
Knap doun capounis of the best   but in the byre –
Heir is bot hamelie fair –   do beliue, Gill'!
Twa cant knaifis of his awin   haistelie he bad,
'The ane of ȝow my capill ta,
The vther his coursour alswa –
To the stabill swyith ȝe ga'!
Than was þe king glaid.

98 gle] the gle L
108 farne] *for authorial* farin

10.

The coilȝear, gudlie in feir,   tuke him be the hand
And put him befoir him,   as ressoun had bene.
Quhen thay come to the dure,   the king begouth to stand,
To put the coilȝear in befoir   maid him to mene.
He said, ‘Thow art vncourtes;   that sall I warrand’.
He tyt the king be the nek,   twa part in tene:
‘Gif thow at bidding suld be   boun or obeysand,
And gif thow of courtasie couth,   thow hes forȝet it clene.
Now is anis’, said the coilȝear.   ‘Kynd aucht to creip,
Sen ellis thow art vnknawin
To mak me lord of my awin.
Sa mot I thriue, I am thrawin;
Begin we to threip’.

11.

Than benwart thay ȝeid,   quhair brandis was bricht,
To ane bricht-byrnand fyre   as the carll bad.
He callit on Gyliane his wyfe   thair supper to dicht,
‘Of the best that thair is...
[portions of three lines missing, one completely]
...help that we had,
Efter ane euill day   to haue ane mirrie nicht.
For sa troublit with stormis   was I neuer stad –
Of ilk airt of the eist   sa laithly it laid.
Ȝit was I mekle willar than
Quhen I met with this man’. sig. [A iv^{r}]
Of sic taillis thay began
Quhill þe supper was graid.

12.

Sone was the supper dicht   and the fyre bet
And thay had weschin, iwis,   the worthiest was thair.
‘Tak my wyfe be the hand   in-feir withoutin let
And gang begin the buird’,   said the coilȝear.
‘That war vnsemand forsuith,   and thyself vnset’;
The king profferit him to gang   and maid ane strange fair.
‘Now is twyse’, said the carll;   ‘me think thow hes forȝet’.

He leit gyrd to the king   withoutin ony mair
And hit him vnder the eir   with his richt hand,
Quhill he stakkerit thairwithall
Half the breid of the hall;
He fain[e] neuer of ane fall
Quhill he the eird fand.

13.

He start vp stoutly agane –   vneis micht he stand –
For anger of that outray   that he had thair tane.
He callit on Gyliane his wyfe,   'Ga! Tak him be the hand
And gang agane to the buird   quhair ȝe suld air haue gane.
Schir, thow art vnskilfull   and that sall I warrand.
Thow byrd to haue nurtour aneuch,   and thow hes nane;
Thow hes walkit, iwis,   in mony wyld land;
The mair vertew thow suld haue   to keip the fra blame.
Thow suld be courtes of kynd   and ane cunnand courteir.
Thocht that I simpill be,
Do as I bid the
The hous is myne, pardie,
And all that is heir'.

14.

The king said to himself,   'This is ane euill lyfe.
Ȝit was I neuer in my lyfe   thus-gait[is] leird,
And I haue oft-tymes bene   quhair gude hes bene ryfe,
That maist couth of courtasie   in this Cristin eird.
Is nane sa gude as leif of   and mak na mair stryfe,
For I am stonischit at this straik   that hes me thus steird'.   sig. [A iv^{v}]
In-feir fairlie he foundis   with the gude-wyfe
Quhair the coilȝear bad,   sa braithlie he beird.
Quhen he had done his bidding   as him gude thocht,
Doun he sat the king neir
And maid him glaid and gude cheir
And said, 'ȝe ar welcum heir
Be him þat me bocht'.

153 faine] faind L
169 thus-gaitis] thus gait L

15.

Quhen thay war seruit   and set to the suppar,
Gyll and the gentill king   Charlis of micht,
Syne on the tother syde   sat the coilȝear.
Thus war thay marschellit but mair   and matchit that nicht.
Thay brocht breid to the buird   and braun of ane bair,
And the worthyest wyne   went vpon hicht.
Thay beirnis, as I wene,   thay had aneuch thair
Within that burelie bigging,   byrnand full bricht.
Syne enteris thair daynteis on deis   dicht dayntelie.
Within that worthie wane
Forsuith wantit thay nane.
With blyith cheir sayis Gyliane,
'Schir, dois glaidlie'.

16.

The carll carpit to the king   cumlie and cleir,
'Schir, the forestaris forsuith   of this forest
Thay haue me all at inuy   for dreid of the deir;
Thay threip that I thring doun   of the fattest.
Thay say I sall to Paris,   thair to compeir
Befoir our cumlie king,   in dule to be drest.
Sic manassing thay me mak   forsuith ilk[ane] ȝeir,
And ȝit aneuch sall I haue   for me and ane gest.
Thairfoir sic as thow seis,   spend on and not spair'.
Thus said gentill Charlis the mane
To the coilȝear agane:
'The king himself hes bene fane
Sumtyme of sic fair'.

17.

Of capounis and cunningis   thay had plentie
With wyne at thair will   and eik vennysoun,   sig. B i[r]
Byrdis bakin in breid,   the best that may be.
Thus full freschlie thay fure   into fusioun.
The carll with ane cleir voce   carpit on he,

200 ilkane] ilk L

Said, 'Gyll, lat the cup raik for my bennysoun
And gar our gaist begin, + syne drink thow to me.
Sen he is ane stranger, me think it ressoun'.
Thay drank dreichlie about, thay wosche and thay rais;
The king with ane blyith cheir
Thankit the coilȝeir.
Syne all the thre into feir
To the fyre gais.

18.

Quhen thay had maid thame eis the coilȝear tald
Mony sindrie taillis efter suppair.
Ane bricht-byrnand fyre was byrnand full bald.
The king held gude countenance and company bair,
And euer to his asking ane answer he ȝald,
Quhill at the last he began to frane farthermair,
'In faith, freind, I wald wit, tell gif ȝe wald,
Quhair is thy maist wynning'? said the coilȝear.
'Out of weir', said the king, 'I wayndit neuer to tell;
With my lady the quene
In office maist haue I bene
All thir ȝeiris fyftene,
In the court for to dwell'.

19.

'Quhat kin office art thow in quhen thow art at hame,
Gif thow dwellis with the quene, proudest in pane'?
'Ane chyld of hir chalmer, schir, be Sanct Iame,
And thocht myself it say, maist inwart of ane.
For my dwelling tonicht I dreid me for blame'.
'Quhat sal I cal þe', said þe coilȝear, 'quhen thow art hyne gane'?
'Wymond of the wardrop is my richt name.
Quhaireuer thow findis me befoir the, þi harberie is tane;
And thow will cum to the court, this I vnderta:
Thow sall haue for thy fewaill sig. [B iv]
For my saik the better saill
And onwart to thy trauaill
Worth ane laid or twa'.

213 syne] and syne L

20.

He said, 'I haue na knawledge quhair the court lyis
And I am wonder wa to cum quhair I am vnkend'.
'And I sall say thee the suith on ilk syde, iwis,
That thow sall wit weill aneuch, or I fra the wend.
Baith the king and the quene meitis in Paris
For to hald thair Ȝule togidder, for scho is efter send.
Thair may thow sell be ressoun als deir as thow will prys,
And ȝit I sall help the, gif + ocht may amend,
For I am knawin with officiaris. In cais thow cum thair,
Haue gude thocht on my name
And speir gif I be at hame,
For I suppois, be Sanct Iame,
Thow sall the better fair'.

21.

'Me think it ressoun, be the rude, that I do thy rid,
In cais I cum to the court and knaw bot the ane.
Is nane sa gude as drink and gang to our bed,
For als far as I wait the nicht is furth gane'.
To ane preuie chalmer beliue thay him led
Quhair ane burely bed was wrocht in that wane,
Closit with courtingis and cumlie cled.
Of the worthiest wyne wantit thay nane;
The coilȝear and his wyfe baith with him thay ȝeid
To serue him all at thay mocht
Till he was in bed brocht.
Mair the king spak nocht,
Bot thankit þame þair deid.

22.

Vpon the morne airlie, quhen it was day,
The king buskit him sone with scant of squyary.
Wachis and wardroparis all war away
That war wont for to walkin mony worthy.

253 ocht] I ocht L
265 cumly] *for authorial* cumlye (*or* cumlyly)

Ane pauyot preuilie brocht him his palfray; sig. B iir
The king thocht lang of this lyfe and lap on in hy.
Than callit he on the carll anent quhair he lay;
For to tak his leif than spak he freindly.
Than walkinnit thay baith and hard he was thair;
The carll start vp sone
And prayit him to abyde none:
'Quhill thir wickit wedderis be done,
I rid nocht ȝe fair'.

23.

'Sa mot I thriue', said the king; 'me war laith to byde.
Is not the morne Ȝule-day, formest of the ȝeir?
Ane man that office suld beir betyme at this tyde
He will be found in his fault that wantis, foroutin weir.
I se the firmament fair vpon ather syde;
I will returne to the court quhill the wedder is cleir.
Call furth the gude-wyfe; lat pay hir or we ryde
For the worthie harberie that I haue fundin heir'.
'Lat be! God forbid', the coilȝear said,
'And thow of Charlis cumpany,
Cheif king of cheualry,
That for ane nichtis harbery
Pay suld be laid'.

24.

'Ȝea, sen it is sa that thow will haue na pay,
Cum the morne to the court and do my counsall.
Deliuer the and bring ane laid and mak na delay;
Thow may not schame with thy craft, gif thow thriue sall.
Gif I may help the ocht to sell, forsuith I sall assay,
And als myself wald haue sum of the fewall'.
'Peter', he said, 'I sall preif the morne, gif I may,
To bring coillis to the court to se gif thay sell sall'.
'Se that thow let nocht, I pray the', said the king.
'In faith', said the coilȝear,
'Traist weill I sal be thair,
For thow will neuer gif the mair
To mak ane lesing.

25.

'Bot tell me now lelely   quhat is thy richt name?   sig. [B ii^{v}]
I will forȝet the morne,   and ony man me greif'.
'Wymond of the wardrop,   I bid not to lane.
Tak gude tent to my name,   the court gif thow will preif;
That I haue said I sall hald,   and that I tell the plane'.
'Quhair ony coilȝear may enchaip   I trow till encheif'.
Quhen he had grantit him to cum,   than was the king fane
And withoutin ony mair let,   than he tuke his leif.
Than the coilȝear had greit thocht   on the cunnand + maid,
Went to the charcoill in hy
To mak his chauffray reddy;
Agane the morne airly
He ordanit him ane laid.

26.

The lyft lemit vp beliue,   and licht was the day;
The king had greit knawledge   the countrie to ken.
Schir Rolland and Oliuer come   rydand the way,
With thame ane thousand and ma   of fensabill men,
War wanderand all the nicht ouir   and mony ma than thay.
On ilk airt outwart   war ordanit sic ten.
Gif thay micht heir of the king   or happin quhair he lay
To Iesus Christ thay pray   that grace thame to len.
Als sone as Schir Rolland   saw it was the king,
He kneillit doun in the place,
Thankand God ane greit space.
Thair was ane meting of grace
At that gaddering.

27.

The gentill knicht Schir Rolland   he kneilit on his kne,
Thankand greit God   that mekill was of micht,
Schir Oliuier at his hand   and bischoppis thre,
Withoutin commounis that come,   and mony vther knicht.
Than to Paris thay pas   all that cheualrie

319 maid] he had maid L

Betuix none of the day and [the] Ȝule-nicht.
The gentill bischop Turpine cummand thay se
With threttie conuent of preistis reuest at ane sicht,
Preichand of prophecie in processioun. sig. B iii[r]
Efter thame, baith fer and neir,
Folkis following in-feir,
Thankand God with gude cheir
Thair lord was gane to toun.

28.

Quhen thay princis appeirit into Paris,
Ilk rew ryallie with riches thame arrayis.
Thair was digne seruice done at Sanct Dyonys
With mony proud prelat, as the buik sayis.
Syne to supper thay went within the palys;
Befoir that mirthfull man menstrallis playis.
Mony wicht wyfis sone, worthie and wise,
Was sene at that semblay ane and twentie dayis,
With all kin principall plentie for his plesance.
Thay callit it the best Ȝule than
And maist worthie began
Sen euer king Charlis was man,
Or euer was in France.

29.

Than vpon the morne airlie quhen the day dew,
The coilȝear had greit thocht quhat he had vndertane.
He kest twa creillis on ane capill with coillis anew,
Wandit thame with widdeis to wend on that wane.
'Mary! It is not my counsall, bot ȝone man that ȝe knew,
To do ȝow in his gentrise', said Gyliane.
'Thow gaif him ane outragious blaw and greit boist blew;
In faith, thow suld haue bocht it deir, and [ȝ]he had bene allane.
Forthy hald ȝow fra the court for ocht that may be.
Ȝone man that thow outrayd

342 the Ȝule] Ȝule L
368 said] *for authorial* saide
370 ȝhe] he L

Is not sa simpill as he said.
Thairun – my lyfe dar I layd –
That sall thow heir and se'.

30.

'Ȝea, dame, haue nane dreid   of my lyfe today;
Lat me wirk as I will –   the weird is mine awin.
I spak not out of ressoun,   the suith gif I sall say,
To Wymond of the wardrop,   war the suith knawin. sig. [B iiiv]
That I haue hecht I sall hald,   happin as it may,
Quhiddersa it gang,   to greif or to gawin'.
He caucht twa creillis on ane capill   and catchit on his way
Ouir the daillis sa derf   be the day was dawin,
The hieway to Paris   in all that he mocht;
With ane quhip in his hand
Cantlie on catchand
To fulfill his cunnand
To the court socht.

31.

Graith thocht of the grant   had the gude king
And callit Schir Rolland him till   and gaif commandment,
Ane man he traistit in maist   atour all vther thing,
That neuer wald set him on assay   withoutin his assent.
'Tak thy hors and thy harnes   in the morning;
For to watche weill the wayis   I wald that thow went.
Gif thow meitis ony leid   lent on the ling,
Gar thame boun to this burgh – I tell the mine intent –,
Or gif thow seis ony man   cumming furth the way,
Quhatsumeuer that he be
Bring him haistely to me,
Befoir none that I him se
In this hall the day'.

32.

Schir Rolland had greit ferly   and in hart kest
Quhat that suld betakin   that the king tald:
Vpon solempnit Ȝule-day,   quhen ilk man suld rest,
That him behouit neidlingis   to watche on the wald,
Quhen his God to serue   he suld haue him drest.
And syne with ane blyith cheir   buskit that bald;
Out of Paris proudly   he preikit full prest
Intill his harnes all haill   his hechtis for to hald.
He vmbekest the countrie   outwith the toun:
H[e] saw nathing on steir,
Nouther fer nor neir,
Bot the feildes in-feir,
Daillis and doun.

33.

He huit and he houerit   quhill midmorne and mair,   sig. [B iv[r]]
Behaldand the hie hillis   and passage sa plane.
Sa saw he quhair the coilȝear   come with all his fair,
With twa creillis on ane capill;   thairof was he fane.
He followit to him haistely   amang the holtis hair
For to bring him to the king   at bidding full bane.
Courtesly to the knicht   kneillit the coilȝear,
And Schir Rolland himself   salust him agane,
Syne bad him leif his courtasie   and boun him to ga.
He said, 'Withoutin letting
Thow mon to Paris to the king;
Speid the fast in ane ling,
Sen I find na ma'.

34.

'In faith', said the coilȝear,   'ȝit was I neuer sa nyse.
Schir knicht, it is na courtasie   commounis to scorne;
Thair is mony better than I   cummis oft to Parys
That the king wait not of,   nouther nicht nor morne.

411 He] Ha L
428 neuer] *for authorial* ne'er

For to towsill me or tit me, thocht foull be my clais,
Or I be dantit on sic wyse, my lyfe sal be lorne'.
'Do way', said Schir Rolland; 'me think thow art not wise.
I rid thow at bidding be, be all that we haue sworne,
And call thow it na scorning, bot do as I the ken,
Sen thow hes hard mine intent:
It is the kingis commandement.
At this tyme thow suld haue went,
And I had met sic ten'.

35.

'I am bot ane mad man that thow hes heir met;
I haue na myster to matche with maisterfull men,
Fairand ouir the feildis fewell to fet,
And oft fylit my feit in mony foull fen,
Gangand with laidis my gouerning to get.
Thair is mony carll in the countrie thow may nocht ken;
I sall hald that I haue hecht, bot I be hard set,
To Wymond of the wardrop; I wait full weill quhen'.
'Sa thriue I', said Rolland 'it is mine intent sig. [B iv[v]]
That nouther to Wymond nor Will
Thow sall hald nor hecht till,
Quhill I haue brocht the to fulfill
The kingis commandment'.

36.

The carll beheld to the knicht as he stude than.
He bair, grauit in gold and gowlis in grene,
Glitterand full gaylie quhen glemis began,
Ane tyger ticht to ane tre, ane takin of tene.
Trewlie that tenefull was trimland than,
Semelie schapin and schroud in that scheild schene.
Mekle worschip of weir worthylie he wan
Befoir into fechting with mony worthie sene.
His basnet was bordourit and burneist bricht

458 trimland] *for authorial* trimeland *or* trimlande
462 burneist] *for authorial* burnischit

With stanis of beriall deir,
Dyamountis and sapheir,
Riche rubeis in-feir
Reulit full richt.

37.

His plaitis properlie picht attour   with precious stanis
And his pulanis full prest   of that ilk peir,
Greit graipis of gold   his greis for the nanis,
And his cussanis cumlie   schynand full cleir;
Bricht braissaris of steill   about his arme-banis
Blandit with beriallis   and cristallis cleir,
Ticht ouir with thopas   and trewlufe at anis –
The teind of his [i]ewellis   to tell war full teir.
His sadill circulit and set   richt sa on ilk syde,
His brydill bellisand and gay;
His steid stout on stray.
He was the ryallest of array
On ronsy micht ryde.

38.

Of that ryall array   that Rolland in raid
Rauf rusit in his hart   of that ryall thing.
'He is the gayest in geir   that euer on ground glaid;
Haue he grace to the gre   in ilk iornaying! sig. C i[r]
War he ane manly man,   as he is weill maid,
He war full michtie with magre   durst abyde his meting'.
He bad the coilȝear in wraith,   'Swyth, withoutin baid,
Cast the creillis fra the capill   and gang to the king'.
'In faith, it war greit schame',   said the coilȝear.
'I vndert[u]k thay suld be brocht
This day for ocht that be mocht;
Schir knicht, that word is for nocht
That thow carpis thair.

474 iewellis] tewellis L
489 vndertuk] vndertak L

39.

Thow huifis on thir holtis   and haldis me heir
Quhill half the haill day   may the hicht haue'.
'Be Christ that was cristinnit   and his mother cleir
Thow sall catche to the court;   that sall not be to craue.
It micht be preifit preiudice,   bot gif thow suld compeir
To se quhat granting of grace   the king wald the gaif.
For na gold on this ground   wald I, but weir,
Be fundin fals to the king,   sa Christ me saue,
To gar the cum and be knawin   as I am command.
I wait not quhat his willis be,
Nor he namit na mair the
Nor ane-vther man to me,
Bot quhome that I fand'.

40.

'Thow fand me sechand nathing   that followit to feid –
I war ane fule gif I fled   and fand nane affray –
Bot as ane lauchfull man   my laidis to leid,
That leifis with mekle lawtie   and laubour, in fay.
Be the mother and the maydin   that maid vs remeid,
And thow mar me ony mair,   cum efter quhatsa may,
Thow and I sall dyntis deill   quhill ane of vs be deid
For the deidis thow hes me done   vpon this deir day'.
Mekle merwell of that word   had Schir Rolland;
He saw na wappinis thair
That the coilȝear bair
Bot ane auld buklair
And ane roustie brand.

41.

'It is lyke', said Schir Rolland   and lichtly he leuch, sig. [C i^{v}]
'That sic ane stubill husbandman   wald stryke stoutly.
Thair is mony toun-man   to tuggill is full teuch,
Thocht thair brandis be blak   and vnburely;
Oft fair foullis ar fundin   faynt and als freuch.
I defend we fecht   or fall in that foly;
Lat se how we may disseuer   with sobernes aneuch

And catche crabitnes away,   be Christ counsall I.
Quhair winnis that Wymond   thow hecht to meit today'?
'With the quene tauld he me,
And thair I vndertuke to be
Into Paris, pardie,
Withoutin delay'.

42.

'And I am knawin with the quene',   said schir Rolland,
And with mony byrdis in hir bowre,   be buikis and bellis.
The king is into Paris –   that sall I warrand –
And all his a[nh]ertance   that in his court dwellis.
Me tharth haue nane noy   of myne erand,
For me think thow will be thair   efter, as thow tellis,
Bot gif I fand the forrow now,   to keip my cunnand'.
'Schir knicht', said þe coilȝear,   'thow trowis me neuer ellis,
Bot gif sum suddand let   put it of delay.
For that I hecht of my will,
And na man threit me thairtill,
That I am haldin to fulfill
And sall do quhill I may'.

43.

'Ȝea, sen thow will be thair   thy cunnandis to new,
I neid nane airar myne erand   nor none of the day'.
'Be thow traist', said the coilȝear,   'man as I am trew,
I will not haist me ane fute   faster on the way.
Bot gif thow raik out of my renk,   full raith sall thow rew
Or be the rude, I sall rais   thy ryall array.
Thocht thy body be braissit   in that bricht hew,
Thow sal be fundin als febill   of thy bone fay'.
Schir Rolland said to himself,   'This is bot foly   sig. C ii[r]
To striue with him ocht mair;
I se weill he will be thair'.
His leif at the coilȝear
He tuke lufesumly.

534 anhertance] aduertance L

44.

'Be Christ', said the coilȝear,   'that war ane foull scorne
That thow suld chaip bot I the knew,   that is sa schynand.
For thow seis my weidis ar auld   and all toworne,
Thow trowis nathing thir taillis   that I am telland.
Bring na beirnis vs by,   bot as we war borne
And thir blonkis that vs beiris;   thairto I mak ane + band
That I sall meit the heir   vpon this mure tomorne,
Gif I be haldin in heill –   and thairto my hand –
Sen that we haue na laiser   at this tyme to ta'.
In ane thourtour way
Seir gaitis pas thay,
Baith to Paris in fay;
Thus partit thay twa.

45.

The gentill knicht Schir Rolland   come rydand full sone
And left the coilȝear to cum   as he had vndertane.
And quhen he come to Paris   the hie mes was done;
The king with mony cumly   out of the kirk is gane.
Of his harnes in hy   he hynt withoutin hone
And in ane rob him arrayit,   richest of ane.
In that worschipfull weid   he went in at none,
As he was wont, with the wy   that weildit the wane,
On fute ferly in-feir   formest of all.
Richt weill payit was the king
Of Schir Rollandis cumming;
To speir of his tything
Efter him gart call.

46.

The king in counsall him callit,   'Cum hidder, schir knicht.
Hes thow my bidding done,   as I the command'?
'In faith', said Schir Rolland,   'I raid on full richt
To watche wyselie the wayis –   that I sall warrand.   sig. [C ii^{v}]

559 all] *for authorial* alle
562 band] bland L

Thair wald na douchtie this day for iornay be dicht;
Fairand ouir the feildis full few thair I fand.
Saif anerly ane man that semblit in my sicht,
Thair was na leid on lyfe lent in this land'.
'Quhat kin a fallow was that ane, schir, I the pray'?
'A man in husband-weid
Buskit busteously on breid;
Leidand coillis he ȝeid
To Paris the way'.

47.

'Quhy hes thow not that husband brocht, as I the bad?
I dreid me, sa he dantit the thow durst not with him deill'.
'In faith', said Schir Rolland, 'gif that he sa had,
That war full hard to my hart, and I ane man in heill'!
He saw the king was engreuit and [f]urth gat glaid
To se gif the coilȝearis lawtie was leill.
'I suld haue maid him in the stour to be full hard stad,
And I had wittin that the carll wald away steill,
Bo[t] I trowit not the day that he wald me beget'.
As he went outwart bayne,
He met ane porter-swayne,
Cummand raith him agayne
Fast fra the ȝet.

48.

'Quhair gangis thow, gedling, thir gaitis sa gane'?
'Be God', said the grome, 'ane gift heir I geif –
I deuise at the ȝet thair is ane allane;
Bot he be lattin in beliue, him lykis not to leif.
With ane capill and twa creillis cassin on the plane,
To cum to this palice he preissis to preif'.
'Gi[f] thow hes fundin that freik, in faith I am fane;

600 furth gat] gat furth L
604 Bot] Bo L
615 Gif] Git L

Lat him in glaidly –   it may not engreif.
Bot askis he eirnestly   efter ony man'?
Than said that gedling on ground,
'Ȝe, forsuith in this stound
Efter ane Wymound
In all that he can'.

49.

'Pas agane, porter,   and lat him swyith in   sig. C iii[r]
Amang the proudest in preis,   plesand in pane.
Say thow art not worthy   to Wymond to win;
Bid him seik him hisself,   gif thair be sic ane'.
Agane gangis Schir Rolland   quhair gle suld begin,
And the ȝaip ȝeman   to the ȝet is gane,
[V]nbraissit the bandis beliue   or that he wald blin,
Syne leit the wy at his will   wend in the wane.
'Gang seik him now thyself',   he said vpon hicht;
'Myself hes na lasair
Fra thir ȝettis to fair'.
'Be Christ', said the coilȝear,
'I set that bot licht.

50.

'Gif thow will not seik him,   my awin self sall,
For I haue oft-tymes swet   in seruice full sair.
Tak keip to my capill   that na man him call
Quhill I cum fra the court',   said the coilȝear.
'My laid war I laith to lois;   I leif the heir all.
Se that thow leis thame not,   bot ȝeme thame full ȝair'.
In that hardy in hy   he haikit to that hall
For to wit gif Wymondis   wynning was thair.
He arguit with the ischar   ofter than anis:
'Schir, can thow ocht say
Quhair is Wymond the day?
I pray the bring him, gif thow may,
Out of this wanis'.

628 Vnbraissit] Enbraissit L

51.

\+ That the wy had wittin   of Wymond he wend,
Bot to his raifand word   he gaue na rewaird.
Thair was na man thairin   that his name kend;
Thay countit not the coilȝear   almaist at regaird.
He saw thair was na meiknes   nor mesure micht mend.
He sped him in spedely   and nane of thame he spaird;
Thair was na fyue of thay freikis   þat micht him furth fend –
He socht in sa sadly   quhill sum of thame he saird.
He thristit in throw thame   thraly with thre[i]t.   sig. [C iiiv]
Quhen he come amang thame all,
Ȝit was the king in the hall
And mony gude man withall
Vngane to the meit.

52.

Thocht he had socht sic ane sicht   all this seuin ȝeir,
Sa solempnit ane semblie   had he not sene.
The hall was properly appe[rr]ellit   and paintit but peir,
Dyamountis full dantely   dentit betwene.
It was semely set   on ilk syde seir,
Gowlis glitterand full gay   glemand in grene,
Flowris with flour-de-lycis   formest in-feir,
With mony flamand ferly,   ma than fyftene.
The rufe reulit about   in reuall of reid,
Rois reulit ryally,
Columbyn and lely.
Thair was ane hailsum harbery
Into riche steid.

53.

With dosouris to the duris dicht,   quhasa wald deme;
With all diuers danteis   dicht dantely,
Circulit with siluer   semely to sene.

648 That] He trowit that L
656 threit] threttis L
663 apperrellit] appectellit L

Selcouthly in seir   [thir] was set suttelly:
Blyth byrdis abufe   and bestiall full bene,
Fyne foullis in fryth   and fischis with fry.
The flure carpit[it] and cled   and couerit full clene,
Cummand fra the cornellis,   closand quemely;
Bricht bancouris about   browdin ouirall.
Greit squechonis on hicht,
Anamalit and weill dicht,
Reulit at all richt
Endlang the hall.

54.

'Heir is ryaltie', said Rauf,   'aneuch for the nanis,
With all nobilnes anournit,   and that is na nay.
Had I of Wymond ane word,   I wald of thir wanis,
Fra thir wyis, iwis,   to went on my way.   sig. [C iv^{r}]
Bot I mon ȝit heir mair   quhat worthis of him anis
And eirnestly efter him   haue myne e ay'.
He thristit in throw   threttie all at anis,
Quhair mony douchtie of deid   war ioynit that day.
For he was vnburely   on bak thay him hynt.
As he gat ben throw,
He gat mony greit schow,
Bot he was stalwart, I trow,
And laith for to stynt.

55.

He thristit in throw thame   and thraly can thring;
Fast to the formest   he foundit in feir.
Sone besyde him he gat ane sicht   of the nobill king.
'Ȝone is Wymond I wait;   it worthis na weir.
I ken him weill thocht he be cled   in vther clething –
In clais of clene gold   kythand ȝone cleir...
  [missing line]
Quhen he harbreit with me   be half as he is heir;

677 thir] he L
680 carpitit] carpit L
681 closand] *for authorial* closande

In faith, he is of mair stait   than euer he me tald!
Allace, that I was hidder wylit;
I dreid me sair I be begylit'.
The king preuilie smylit
Quhen he saw that bald.

56.

Thair was seruit in that saill   seigis semelie,
Mony senȝeorabill syre   on ilk syde seir.
With ane cairfull countenance   the coilȝear kest his e
To the cumly quene,   courtes and cleir:
'Dame, of thy glitterand gyde   haue I no gle,
Be the gracious God   that bocht vs sa deir.
To ken kingis courtasie   the deuill come to me,
And sa I hope I may say   or I chaip heir.
Micht I chaip of this chance   that changes my cheir,
Thair suld na man be sa wyse
To gar me cum to Parise
To luke quhair the king lyis –
In faith, this seuin ȝeir'.

57.

Quhen worthie had weschin   and fra the buirdis went,   sig. [C iv^{v}]
Thay war forwonderit, iwis,   of thair wyse lord.
The king fell in carping   and tauld his intent;
To mony gracious grome   he maid his record,
How the busteous beirne   met him on the bent
And how the frostis war sa fell   and sa strait ford.
Than the coilȝear quoke   as he had bene schent,
Quhen he hard the suith say   how he the king schord:
'Greit God, gif I war now   and thyself withall
Vpon the mure quhair we met,
Baith all suddandly set,
Or ony knicht that thow may get
Sa gude in thy hall'!

58.

Thir lordis leuch vpon loft   and lystinit to the king,
How he was ludgeit and led   and set at sa licht.
Than the curagious knichtis bad,   'Haue him to hing,
For he hes seruit that',   thay said, 'be our sicht'.
'God forbot', he said,   'my thank war sic thing
To him that succourit my lyfe   in sa + ill ane nicht!
Him semis ane stalwart man   and stout in stryking;
That carll for his courtasie   sal be maid knicht.
I hald the counsall full euill   that Cristin man slais,
For I had myster to haue ma
And not to distroy tha
Tha[t] war worthie to ga
To fecht on Goddis fais'.

59.

Befoir mony worthie   he dubbit him knicht,
Dukis and digne lordis   in that deir hall.
'Schir, se for thyself;   thow semis to be wicht.
Tak keip to this ordour;   ane knicht I the call.
To mak the manly man,   I mak the of micht:
Ilk ȝeir thre hundreth pund   assigne the I sall,
And als the nixt vacant   be ressonabill richt
That hapnis in France;   quhairsaeuer it fall,
Forfaitour or fre waird   that first cummis to hand   sig. D i^{r}
I gif the heir heritabilly,
Sa that I heir quhen I haue hy
That thow be fundin reddy
With birny and brand.

60.

'It war my will, worthy,   thy schone that thow wan
And went with thir weryouris,   wythest in weir.
Heir ar curagious knichtis,   suppois thay the nocht ken
For thy simpill degre   that thow art in heir.

743 ill] euill L
749 That] Tha L

I beseik God of his grace   to mak the ane gude man,
And I sall gif the to begin   glitterand geir'.
Ane chalmer with armour   the king gart richt than,
Betaucht to ane squyar   and maid him keipeir,
With clois armouris of steill   for that stout knicht;
Sextie squyaris of fee
Of his retinew to be.
That was ane fair cumpany
Schir Rauf gat that nicht.

61.

Vpon the morne airly   Schir Rauf wald not rest,
Bot in ryall array   he reddyit him to ryde.
'For to hald that I haue hecht   I hope it be the best,
To ȝone busteous beirne   that boistit me to byde.
Amang thir galȝart gromis,   I am bot ane gest;
I will the ganandest gait   to that gay glyde.
Sall neuer lord lauch on loft   quhill my lyfe may lest
That I for liddernes suld leif,   and leuand besyde!
It war ane graceles gude   that I war cummin to,
Gif that the king hard on hicht
That he had maid ane carll knicht
Amang thir weryouris wicht,
And docht nocht to do'!

62.

Vpon ane rude runsy   he ruschit out of toun;
In ane ryall array   he rydis full richt.
Euin to the montane   he maid him full boun
Quhair he had trystit to meit   Schir Rolland the knicht,   sig. [D iv]
Derfly ouir daillis,   discouerand the doun
Gif ony douchtie that day   for iornayis was dicht.
He band his blonk to ane busk   on the bent broun,
Syne baid be the bair way   to hald that he had hecht,
Quhill it was neir time of the day   that he had thair bene.
He lukit ane lytill him fra;
He saw cummand in thra
The maist man of all tha
That euer he had sene.

63.

Ane knicht on ane cameill come   cantly at hand
With ane curagious countenance   and cruell to se.
He semit baldly to abyde   with birny and with brand;
His blonk was vnburely,   braid and ouir-hie.
Schir Rauf reddyit him sone   and come rydand,
And in the rowme of ane renk   in fewtir kest he –
He semit fer fellonar   than first quhen he him fand.
He foundis, throw his forcenes   gif he micht him se;
He straik the steid with the spurris;   he sprent on the bent.
Sa hard ane cours maid thay
That baith thair hors deid lay;
Thair speiris in splenders away
Abufe thair heid sprent.

64.

Thus war thay for thair forcynes   left on fute baith;
Thay sture hors, at that straik   strikin, deid lay than.
Thir riche restles renkis   ruschit out full raith,
Cleikit out twa swordis   and togidder ran,
Kest thame with gude will   to do vther skaith,
Bait on thair basnetis   thay beirnes, or thay blan.
Haistely hewit thay togidder;   to leif thay war laith
To tyne the worschip of weir   that thay air wan,
Na for dout of vincussing   thay went nocht away.
Thus ather vther can assaill
With swordis of mettaill;
Thay maid ane lang battall,
Ane hour of the day.

65.

Thay hard-harnest men   thay hewit on in haist –   sig. D ii^{r}
Thay worthit heuy with heid   and angerit withall –
Quhill thay had maid thame sa mait   thay failȝe almaist,
Sa laith thay war on ather part   to lat thair price fall.
The riche restles men   out of the renk past,
Forwrocht with thair wapnis   and euill rent withall.
Thair was na girth on the ground,   quihill ane gaif þe gaist;

Ȝarne efter ȝeilding on ilk syde thay call.
Schir Rauf caucht to cule him and tak mair of the licht;
He kest vp his veseir
With ane cheualrous cheir.
Sa saw he cummand full neir
Ane-vther kene knicht.

66.

'Now be the rude', said Schir Rauf, 'I repreif the!
Thow hes brokin conditioun; thow hes not done richt!
Thow hecht na bak heir to bring, bot anerly we;
Thairto I tuik thy hand, as thow was trew knicht'.
On loud said the Sarazine, 'I heir the now lie;
Befoir the same day I saw the neuer with sicht.
Now sall thow think it richt sone thow hes met with me,
Gif Mahoun or Termagant may mantene my micht'!
Schir Rauf was blyth of þat word and blenkit with his face,
'Thow sayis thow art ane Sarazine;
Now thankit be Drichtine
That ane of vs sall neuer hine,
Vndeid in this place'!

67.

Than said the Sarazine to Schir Rauf succudrously,
'I haue na lyking to lyfe to lat the with lufe'!
He gaue ane braid with his brand to the beirne by
Till the blude of his browis brest out abufe.
The kene knicht in that steid stakkerit sturely;
The lenth of ane rude-braid he gart him remufe.
Schir Rauf ruschit vp agane and hit him in hy.
Thay preis furth properly thair pithis to prufe;
Ilkane a schort knyfe braidit out sone. sig. [D ii^{v}]
In stour stifly thay stand
With twa knyfis in hand;
With that come Schir Rolland
As thay had neir done.

842 repreif] *for authorial* repreiue

68.

The gentill knicht Schir Rolland   come rydand ful richt
And ruschit fra his runsy   and ran thame betwene.
He sayis, 'Thow art ane Sarazine,   I se be my sicht,
For to confound our Cristin men   that counteris sa kene.
Tell me thy name tyte,   thow trauelland knicht.
Fy on thy fechting!   Fell hes thow bene.
Thow art stout and strang   and stalwart in fecht;
Sa is thy fallow, in faith,   and that is weill sene.
In Christ and thow will trow,   thow takis nane outray'.
'Forsuith', the Sarazine said,
'Thyself maid me neuer sa affraid
That I for souerance wald haue praid,
Na not sall today.

69.

'Breif me not with ȝour boist,   bot mak ȝow baith boun;
Batteris on baldly   the best, I ȝow pray'.
'Na', said Schir Rolland,   'that war na resoun.
I trow in the mekle God   that maist of michtis may;
The tane is in power   to mak that presoun,
For that war na wassalage,   sum men wald say.
I rid that thow hartfully   forsaik thy Mahoun.
Fy on that foull feind,   for fals is thy fay;
Becum Cristin, schir knicht,   and on Christ call!
It is my will thow conuert –
This wickit warld is bot ane start –
And haue him halely in hart
That maker is of all'.

70.

'Schir Rolland, I rek nocht   of thy rauingis;
Thow dois bot reuerence to thame   that rekkis it nocht.
Thow slane hes oft thyself   of my counsingis,
Soudanis and sib-men   that the with schame socht.   sig. [D iii^{r}]
Now faindis to haue fauour   with thy fleichingis;
Now haue I ferlie, gif I   fauour the ocht.
We sall spuilȝe ȝow dispittously   at the nixt springis,

Mak ȝow biggingis full bair – bodword haue I brocht –,
Chace Charlis ȝour king   fer out of France –
Fra the Chane of Tartarie;
At him this message wald I be,
To tell him as I haue tauld the
Withoutin plesance'.

71.

'Tyte tell me thy name   – it seruis of nocht –:
Ȝe Sarazeins ar succuderus   and self-willit ay.
Sall neuer of sa sour ane brand   ane bricht fyre be brocht,
The feynd is sa felloun   als fer as he may'.
'Sa thriue I', said the Sarazine,   'to threip is my thocht.
Quha waitis the Cristin with cair,   my cussingis ar thay;
My name is Magog,   in will, and I mocht,
To ding thame doun dourly   that euer war in my way.
Forthy my warysoun is full gude   at hame quhair I dwel'.
'In faith', said Schir Rolland,
'That is full euill wyn land
To haue quhill thow ar leuand,
Sine at thine end hell.

72.

'Wald thow conuert the in hy   and couer the of sin,
Thow suld haue mair profite   and mekle pardoun,
Riche douchereis seir   to be sesit in,
During quhill day dawis   that neuer will gang doun;
Wed ane worthie to wyfe   and weild hir with win,
Ane of the riche of our realme –   be that ressoun –
The gentill duches Dame Iane –   that clamis be hir kin
Angeos and vther landis   with mony riche toun.
Thus may thow, and thow will,   wirk the best wise;
I do the out of dispair,
In all France is nane so fair.
Als scho is appeirand air
To twa douchereis'.

73.

‘I rek nocht of thy riches, Schir Rolland the knicht’, sig. [D iii^{v}]
Said the rude Sarazine in ryall array.
‘Thy go[l]d nor thy grassum set I bot licht.
Bot gif thy god be sa gude, as I heir the say,
I will forsaik Mahoun and tak me to his micht
Euermair perpetuallie as he that mair may.
Heir with hart and gude will my treuth I the plicht
That I sall lelely leif on thy lord ay,
And I beseik him of grace and askis him mercy,
And Christ his sone full schene.
For I haue Cristin men sene
That in mony angeris hes bene
Full oft on him cry’.

74.

‘I thank God’, said Rolland, ‘that word lykis me,
And Christ, his sweit sone, that the that grace send’.
Thay swoir on thair swordis swyftlie all thre
And conseruit thame freindis to thair lyfis end,
Euer in all trauell to leif and to die; –
Thay knichtis caryit to þe court; – as Christ had þame kend.
The king for thair cumming maid game and gle
With mony mirthfull man thair mirthis to mend.
Digne bischoppis that day that douchtie gart bring
And gaue him sacramentis seir
And callit him Schir Gawteir,
And sine the duches cleir
He weddit with ane ring.

75.

Than Schir Rauf gat rewaird to keip his knichtheid.
Sic tythingis come to the king within thay nyne nicht
That the marschell of France was newlingis deid.
Richt thair with the counsall of mony kene knicht

935 gold] God L
952 game] *for authorial* gamin

He thocht him richt worthie   to byde in his steid
For to weild that worschip,   worthie and wicht.
His wyfe wald he nocht forȝet   for dout of Goddis feid;
He sent efter that hende   to leif tham in richt,
Syne foundit ane fair place   quhair he met the king, sig. [D iv^{r}]
Euermair perpetually
In the name of Sanct Iuly,
That all that wantis harbery
Suld haue gestning.

F I N I S.

Imprentit at Sanct Androis be Robert Lekpreuik.   Anno 1572.

Notes

2 *flan*: Although the word appears in *DOST* as a unique early usage, there are abundant uses in *SND* (including a derived verb 'to gust, blow'). Derived from ON *flan* and *flana* v., the OSc uses show sense-specification; the Scandinavian etyma have only the general sense '(to) rush'.

3 *vther mony ane*: Functionally equivalent to *mony ane-vther* 'many another'. Such post-posited modifiers occur frequently in OSc and ME, often, as here, to facilitate rhyme.

4 *fra Sanct Thomas*: Amours is surely right to argue that this is the *fra* of time, not of space (cf. *Gawain* 8); the on-verse thus means, 'turned their course, beginning with the feast of St Thomas [of Inde]', 21 December. In contrast to the traditional thirteen-line alliterative scene, the shameful lordly hunt, The Other to be here confronted is not Death, but a member of another, non-noble class.

16 *sture*: In the print actually *slure*. *DOST sture* adj. (adv.) B offers only a single parallel, from *The Freiris of Berwick*. But the form here represents a common licence widespread in stanzaic poetry; in a clearly parallel construction, a proximate form of the root may stand in for the grammatically appropriate one to provide a rhyme. Other examples occur, for instance, in 20, where *pure* represents *purest*; in the singular *doun* for obvious plural at 413 (cf. *hie hillis* 416); and in the plural form of a normally singular oath at 532; see further 656n and cf. examples from the *Howlat* (discussed at Holland 2014, 49–50). Similarly, the analogous form in *Freiris* also provides a rhyme.

17 *drift*: As every editor since Laing has recognised, the first use of *deip* has been attracted to the use later in the line. I follow Laing's suggested replacement *drift* 'driving snow'. Amours suggested the palaeographically more attractive *drip* 'snow';

but the noun is not found in *DSL*, although recorded in *The English Dialect Dictionary* as a northernism.

durandlie: Cited by *DOST* elsewhere only at *Golagros* 337.

18 In this punctuation, *fure* governs both halves of the line, and the two modifying *sa*'s introduce a result clause. One might alternatively see the a-verse as enjambed from the previous line and provide stronger mid-line punctuation. In 19, *Thair* is probably loosely collocated with later *on*.

20 *proudest and pure*: Implies 'purest' suppressed for the rhyme (cf. 16n). Although I gloss the rhyme-word as the obvious 'pure', a strong case might be made for 'poor(est)'. Such a reading would signal central issues in the poem; in the constraints imposed by circumstance, even the noblest are destitute without aid (a rather distant allusion to the thematic customary in the thirteen-line tradition of death poems) – and, as events will prove, Rauf's outdoor exertions in pursuit of a living, his *mekle vnrufe* 47, might well represent suitably heroic exertions. *men* is otiose and perhaps to be dropped (as also at 871 and 943), since poets, if not those who transmit their materials, are fond of using adjectives absolutely.

21 *wist*: I take this to be a representation of *wiss(c)hit* 'wished', past of *DOST wis* v.1.

27 *on*: Although metrically subordinated, this word carries the alliteration, if such is needed after a potentially triple-rhymed on-verse.

28 *and blew*: Understood in alliterative usage to carry over the prefix from the preceding verb; cf. *Golagros* 628, 'Al tostiffillit and stonayt'. The line alliterates abb|ab, with b-verse stress and rhyme on *-in*.

29 Translate: 'Mid-morning had passed by the time they had variously separated'. The line-ending *was* serves as an auxiliary for both lexical verbs and represents pluperfect 'had', an example of the use, frequent in both ME and OSc, of *to be* (rather than *to have*) as auxiliary with intransitive verbs.

31 *bute bot*: Riddy translates aptly; the line should mean broadly, 'He prayed for succour'. However, that is not what the received text says, and Riddy's rendition, although in accord with *DOST bote* n.1, sense 1b, essentially translates *bot* twice. *DOST* does not record any form parallel to ME *nobot* 'only' (cf. *Gawain* 2182), and metrically *bot* must belong to the b-verse. As Riddy's double-translation signals, this is an example of compositorial haplography, two similar words reproduced as a single one. Like virtually all the clearly recognisable errors in the text (e.g. 17 above), this represents attraction to neighbouring copy.

Given the appeal for divine succour, Rauf's appearance should probably be understood as providential, a foretaste of his inadvertent performance as Christian champion in the poem's final episode. And cf. 330–36. Oaths in the poem, just like contractual promises, carry considerable weight; cf. 45 etc.

34 *braid*: The reflex of OE *brǣdu*, here rhyming with words earlier in ME *ā* as later OSc *ē*. But see also *DOST brade* adj., sense 3 (with a parallel in Wyntoun).

35 *wox he*: The transmitted verse does not meet standard alliterative b-verse syllabic constraints. I have produced a proper metrical form by a simple transposition.

37 *montanis on hicht*: The phrase simply represents a rhyme-constrained version of *montanis hie*.

39–40 Stanza-linking often occurs more or less rigorously in thirteen-line poems. Here its appearance is intermittent, perhaps just an accidental product of the persistent repetitiveness that marks alliterative poetry. There are further examples at 51–53, 64–66, 141–42, 154–55 (rhyme carryover only, but cf. 65–66), 297–98, 333–38, 440–41, 479–80, 505–6, 582–83, 685–87 (especially if one reads *reulit* as representing *raillit*, then echoed in *ryaltie*), possibly 822–29 (!), perhaps 867–68.

40 *lait*: The word means the opposite of what appears, the well-attested sense 'recent(ly)' (*DOST late* adj., sense 3); cf. Henryson's Cresseid as 'lait lipper' (*Testament* 609). Translate, 'that night came upon him so quickly'.

44 *withoutin debait*: Although probably just the relatively empty asseveration, 'There's no denying it', the phrase has been carefully chosen for its proleptic properties, situations in which what appears to one party politeness produces dissension.

54 *thy*: The compositor's form for the intended *thyn*. The line is a normal example of the rhyme-pattern ab|ab, the first rhyme of the b-verse provided by 'slant-alliteration', to be read as *thy n'answer*. Since this is not a substantive, but a spelling-variant, I retain the text as set.

55 *taist*: I follow a suggestion from *DOST traist* v.2; there in one citation, Hay's *Alexander* 14294, *traist* represents *taist* 'test' (or conceivably 'taste'), which seems much to the point. Again, the compositor appears to have been attracted to proximate copy; cf. *trow* in following line. Translate this line and the following: 'Whenever you wish to, test me. For I believe, if I don't always behave so (contextually 'if my answer is not always excellent'), you will bear some responsibility for that' (cf. 'twa part' 123). The episode might be seen as answering well-attested proverbial wisdom, of a sort underlying Gill's hesitancy at 367ff., e.g., 'First to prove [a guest] and syne to trust' (Whiting P429; 1951, 114, s.v. Prove); 'Try before you trust' (Whiting 1951, 146, s.v. Try).

59 *rest*: the reading *reset* 'shelter' is very attractive; parallels occur in the storm scenes of both *Awntyrs* 81 and *Golagros* 38.

61 Translate: 'I would have much greater profit, were I to find a friend'.

66 *at*: Although Scots has *nere-hand* in the appropriate sense, the b-verse is short a syllable. I have adopted the minimal revision to produce a full half-line.

68 The line probably alliterates, rhyming aba|bx with slant-alliteration -*my n'awin*.

70 Following Bradbury, a version of Whiting T15 (1951, 158, s.v. Take): 'Take as one finds'.

72–73 The lines form a parenthetical alternative to *thow* in the preceding line.

74 *sa*: The compositor, attracted to the surrounding alliteration, set *fa*.

81 *meit*: For the rhyme, see the Introduction, p. 9.

86 See Whiting P39 (1951, 108, s.v. Parting).

87 See Whiting L562 (1949, 205, s.v. Love v.2; and cf. L62).

89 *ȝe*: Pronomial usage, alternation between the familiar (implying address of an inferior) and polite forms, is a carefully handled minor source of humour throughout the poem; here Charles momentarily addresses Rauf as if an equal. But contrast his inadvertent, yet offensive fall into the royal *we* at 291.

98 Something has gone wrong with the line, marked by its 'double-dipped' b-verse. Laing and Herrtage read 'was glaid', which is an easier reading and does not address the most overt problem. I have simply assumed that *the*[2] represents dittography after preceding -*th*; removal of this word restores b-verse metricality. But other alternatives are possible. *with* may be part of the a-verse as a complement to *glaid*, although I suspect this reading would involve a more substantial intrusion, replacement of *with* with *furth* or the like.

99 Only the word-order is confusing; translate: 'she never dared be idle when she heard him issue an order', or more directly, 'she never ignored an order that she heard'.

107 *kendill on*: *DOST* offers at least one parallel for the apparently intrusive *on*, Douglas's *Aeneid* 2.6.64.

108 To be metrical, the b-verse requires reading *far[i]n*, an example of a non-substantive change not entered in the text.

109 *Ane ryall rufe het fyre*: The phrase traditionally has elicited editorial commentary, in the main translations like 'A fire so hot it warms to the roof'. The difficulty here is *rufe*, presented as a unique usage in *DOST*. But the spelling provides a plausible derivative of OE *rōf* 'strong, vigorous', i.e., 'a noble (notice the irony), strong, hot fire'. But given the isolation of the form, *rufe* may be adverbial, as if from OE **rōfe*, and *het* not a back-spelling for *hait* but a representation of the past participle *hette* 'heated'. Translate this rendition 'a noble, vigorously lit fire'. See the analysis at *OED rufe* adj., with a supporting citation from the Maitland Folio manuscript.

110 *his*: Simply the neuter possessive ('its'), the antecedent *fyre*.

114 *The ane*: Probably for *The tane*?

126 *Kynd aucht to creip*: This represents but half the conventional proverb, 'Kind ought to creep where it may not go'; see Whiting K34 (1949, 195, s.v. Kynd). Its purport has been missed by every past editor; typical is Speed's mistranslation, 'One's breeding ought to show itself'. This is lexically impossible; *kynd* 'nature' and *courtesy* 'nurture' are not synonyms, but antonyms. For proverbial statements of the distinction, cf. (the opposed) 'Nature passes nurture' and 'He is better fed nor nurtured' (Whiting F107, N25; 1951, 102, s.v. Nature; 105, s.v. Nurtured; the second actually the detritus of a little rhyme, '...fed nor bred').

Whiting cites the relevant analogues: in complicated but explanatory dramatic contexts, the Towneley *Secunda pastorum* 591 and *Everyman* 316, much more succinctly a couplet from MS Rawlinson C.813: 'Kynde will crepe wher itt may nott go, | And shewe ittselfe whens itt came fro'. I would translate the full proverb, 'If you're not strong enough to perform independently (*go*, i.e., walk), you should hold fast to your own kin [your biological *kynd*]' (who supported you when you could only crawl (*creip*) – and implicitly, have the responsibility for doing so again, should you get into difficulties).

This misprision has been stimulated by the difficult wheel. In trying to avoid its problems, past editors have read the proverb backwards, as an appositive to the preceding line. But it appears to me much more likely that one should read forward, taking *Sen* ('since') as dependent upon the proverbial half-line. Such a reading depends on seeing the ambiguity of *vnknawin*, both 'a stranger, someone unknown to me' and, as a result, 'ignorant (of my situation)'. A rough and distant paraphrase: '[If you are going to behave as if you were lord here,] you should go try your "courtesy" on your own folks (who as kin, must accept your behaviour), since you are completely ignorant (*ellis* goes with *vnknawin*) of how I have gathered my estate'. Or a bit more trenchantly, 'As a stranger, you can't honour me with what's mine already' – an independence to be inverted, when Charles will later reveal a way of honouring and augmenting Rauf's hospitality.

In all this discussion, one feature of the proverb – that it is a joke – has been completely lost. Whatever the message Rauf intends, the proverb describes how one should proceed towards some goal, which is, of course, the root of the contention here, a question of proper entry.

128 *make me lord of my own*: As every editor since Amours has pointed out, a comparable line appears at *Golagros* 147, and the sentiment is substantially repeated here at 166–67.

129–30 *I am thrawin*: Translate, 'I am truly angered. We are on the verge of a quarrel'. I wonder, however (especially given *twa part in tene* 123), whether this clause might have originally been a subjunctive, lost in transmission, and the final line of the stanza, with a subject–verb inversion that typifies subjunctive constructions, dependent on its predecessor, 'Were I really to get peevish, we would begin to fight'. This would require seeing *I am* as representing an original *be I*.

132 *bricht-*: This inherently adverbial usage, of course, echoes the adjectival rhyme-word of the preceding line. Cf. further 222, where a similar near repetition is distinguished by use of same word as adjective and participle. The thirteen-line stanza traditionally demands profuse distinctions, most minimally three differing alliterative staves to the line and four different end-rhymes to the stanza. But *Rauf* persistently challenges this formal rule for differentiation, not simply in its frequent generalising diction and through echoic usages like this, but by insistent repetition of rhyme-words within the same stanza. This technique often inherently is a sign of a reciprocity between actors who consider themselves different from their adversaries (e.g., at 806, 808). One particularly flagrant example, a stanza whose longlines are fundamentally monorhymed, occurs at 233–40 (see the Introduction, p. 9 and n.13).

134 The lost materials probably reflect an underlying skip between two uses of *is* at mid-line. As printed, the second half of this line does not seem to follow from the first half.

135 See Whiting D30 (1959, 156, s.v. Day).

136 *troublit*: Given the (unusual for this poem) emphatic /st/-rhyme, a reading like *sa [s]troublit* 'so perturbed' has some attraction. Immediately after *sa*, this might be taken as an example of a compositorial haplography, having written one *s*-, the second example suppressed. See *DOST strubill* v., as well as the much more widely attested *MED stourben* v., *stourblen* v.

137 *laid*: A back-spelling for the past tense 'led'; translate, '[The day] brought storms with such hostility'.

142 *Sone*: 'As soon as' (OE *sōna* 'immediately').

143 The b-verse modifies the subject *thay* in the a-verse.

146 *war*: This auxiliary modifies the lexical verbs in both verses; translate the second: 'if you were (to remain) unseated'.

147 Translate the a-verse: 'The king proposed (to allow) Rauf (= *him*) to go first'.

148 *Now is twyse*: Which rather implies the traditional folk-motif of three trials; cf. *Gawain* 1680 (Whiting T317). The third occasion, which indeed 'pays for all', occurs on Rauf's visit to Charles's court.

153 Browne persuasively interpreted *faind* as 'stopped'. But he failed to notice, just as *DOST faind* pt. does, that *finen* is a strong verb. (Although from French, its forms have been assimilated to common verbs like OE *scīnan* and *hrīnan*; cf. French *strive*, assimilated to *drīfan*.) Although *-d* may be attached by analogy with weak verb forms, it is more likely that the compositor has adjusted the form to match *fand* in the next verse, yet another example of attraction to surrounding copy. With the action here, cf. the proverb 'Who fallis heichest gettis the greitest faw' (Whiting H377; 1949, 189, s.v. High 2).

155 Perhaps obviously, *he* here refers to Charles, but in 157 to Rauf.

158–59 The polite plural *ȝe* addresses both wife and king, but in the next line, Rauf addresses Charles familiarly.

160 *Thow bird*: Although Browne sees the form as an 'anglicisation' and argues that *byrd* should be impersonal and requires line-opening *Th[e]*, see *DOST bird(e)* pt., sense 2 for the sense 'ought'. Contrast the impersonal *him behouit* 405, in the different sense 'it was required of/necessary for him'.

169 The b-verse lacks a syllable of being metrical; the loss is easily repaired, following *DOST thusgatis* adv.

170-71 *gude...That*: Translate 'good men who'.

176 *he*[1]: Refers to the king, while *his* does to Rauf. *him*, however, is ambiguous, particularly following the concatenation of references to *gude* in the stanza. It could refer to either, especially since *he* in the next line refers to Rauf.

182 *Charlis of micht*: Simply a translation of the formal 'Charlemagne'. Cf. *Charlis the Mane* 203. The line probably rhymes aax|ax; cross-rhyme of voiceless /ʧ/ and voiced /ʤ/ occurs at *Gawain* 86: 'He watz so joly of his joyfnes, and sumquat childgered'.

184 *marschellit*: Proleptic; cf. 961, where Rauf's attention to proprieties in his own house (the acts associated with a marshal or steward/seneschal) gains a corresponding reward.

186 *vpon hicht*: Although unrecognised in *DOST*, this is probably *MED highthe* n. 'haste'.

187 *had aneuch*: Cf. 'Aneuch is evin a feist', Whiting E115 (1949, 163, s.v. Enough), also relevant to 201. But given the courses to come, the proverb might be seen as inverted; the episode certainly stands as a counter-demonstration to a proverb like 'A light supper makes a long life' (Whiting S912–13; 1951, 104–5, s.v. Night 5).

196–99 Deer-poaching, the misuse of a property conventionally seen as magnatial, if not royal, plays a prominent role in 'king in disguise' analogues. Here Rauf will perhaps serve Charles 'his own' venison in the next stanza. The king offers an ironic comment on such 'fare' at 205–6, and this canny use of the countryside, rather than Rauf's lese-majesty, may provoke the courtiers' threatened violence at 740–41.

198 *sall*: There is an implied verb of motion; translate, 'I will be obliged to come'.

200 *ilkane*: The b-verse, given normal rules for stress assignment, which would prioritise *-suith*, needs an extra syllable. I have used the form recorded elsewhere in the text.

202 *spend on and not spair*: The collocation of the two verbs (analogous to the ME winner and waster) is widespread and thus, rather naturally, pops up in proverbs; cf. Whiting T316 and particularly S626. The latter, proleptic in this context, appears in the putative source, *John the Reeve*: 'He that never spends but always spares, commonly the worse he fares' (455–57). Cf. also Whiting S628 (1951, 130, s.v. Spend): 'Scarce spending skathis gentrice'.

208 *vennysoun*: Although I gloss the word as the modern 'deer-meat', the term in both ME and OSc has wider application, basically 'game'. It thus might include both *cunningis* (for which in England, at least, one needs a writ granting 'free warren') and *Byrdis* (the victims of lordly falconers).

212 *for my bennysoun*: i.e., 'drink that I may be blessed, to my health'.

213 The b-verse is 'double-dipped' and has an extra syllable. I have dropped *and* as a clarifying insertion and allowed the verse to stand as parallel to the preceding.

215 *dreichlie*: Presented as a unique usage in *DOST*, although a transparent derivative of common *DOST dreich* adj. 'long-lasting'.

220 *coilȝear*: Here the b-verse syllabic rules require that the word be trisyllabic, as again in the same general lexo-syntactic frame at 293.

221 *efter soppair*: To be construed with *at eis* in the preceding line.

224–25 In the first line, *his* = Rauf's, *he* = the king; in 225, *he* = Rauf.

225 *farthermair*: The *DOST* entry suggests the word occurs infrequently, comprehensible, since it means the same thing as the simplex *further*.

229 *my lady*: A sneaky bit of ambiguity, since the word connotes both 'my wife' and 'my mistress'.

235 *be Sanct Iame*: The characters are differentiated by their oaths (cf. Rauf's repeated 'Peter' and 'In faith'). Charlemagne's oath identifies him with Spanish adventurism, an anti-Islamic crusade to 'free' the saint's shrine in Compostela, and emphasises his connection with Roland, while Rauf's alludes to a broader, non-sectarian 'fidelity'.

239 *Wymond*: Although she is not much moved by these earlier suggestions, Walsh offers references to trickster figures called Wymo(u)nd in the romance *Athelston* and the York Plays. See further *MED wi-mount* n.

246 *quhair the court lyis*: While it is an alien venue, Rauf is aware of customary medieval royal practice. Kings were routinely peripatetic and expected their subjects, particularly the greater ones, to provide them with hospitality in their processions through the countryside.

253 Another 'double-dipped' b-verse. I have restored the metrical pattern by suppressing *I*; in this rendition, the subject is implicitly 'it', 'if it can help in any way'. Other solutions are obviously possible, e.g., reading *[m]end* (cf. *mend* 653), or transposing to *may ocht*.

259 *rid*: Rhyme shows that compositor's universal *rid* simply shrouds the expected *reid* (OE *rǣd*).

265 *cumly*: A metrical b-verse requires a trisyllabic word, which this adverb represents; cf. the etymon, OE *cymlīce*, and the trisyllabic usage at *Gawain* 648 (as well as that text's byforms *comlyly* at 360 and 974). *DOST cumly* adv. records one spelling with medial *-e-*, apparently trisyllabic, in Montgomerie's *Flyting*.

271 *deid*: Singular in plural sense for the rhyme.

273 *sone*: One might well emend to the stock phrase *buskit him boun*, which would create a line rhyming aa|bb. This is a synonymous substitution, an error-type widely in evidence, and the compositor may have been attracted by the *s*'s of the off-verse.

276 *pauyot*: Presented in *DOST* as a unique usage.

278 *anent*: *DOST* presents no adverbial forms (conceivably *him* has dropped out), but the sense 'opposite' or 'in front of him' seems clear enough. A handful of late adverbial uses appear in *OED* and (once) in *SND*.

279 *tak*: The usual alliterative collocation here would be *lach his leif*; see *DOST* laught v.1, sense 4 (only recorded in the past and past participle). But this set form is again avoided at 318.

286 *formest of the ȝeir*: There are, of course, a variety of ways of calculating 'the new year' in medieval Britain – from 1 January, by regnal year (beginning with the date of the ruler's coronation), in England from the 'quarter-day' (25 March). But particularly in popular materials (like prophecies for the year), 'mid-winter-day', Christmas is prominent.

288 *found in*: Arguably a small bit of dissimilation, since elsewhere the past participle is represented as *fundin* (cf. 292), and the compositor may have simplified a repetitive sequence.

290 The b-verse is probably metrical, since one might elide either *wedd'ris* or *wedder's*.

291 *we*: At the point of extending, as he thinks, his largesse, Charles uniquely slips into (his accustomed?) 'royal we'.

293 *God forbid*: The sense runs consecutively to 296 *That for*, and the intervening lines succeed, 'especially if you are from among Charles's household...'.

298 One might cf. 'His chance tonicht, it may be thine tomorrow' (Whiting T405; 1951, 143, s.v. Tonight), or 'A kingis word shuld be a kingis bonde' (cf. Whiting W609; 1951, 160, s.v. Word).

300 *deliver*: Identified as a unique usage in *DOST*.

309–10 Translate: 'For you would never make this further offer (i.e., insisting on my carrying through what you offered last night, at 240–54), were you only going to break your word'. The text, in this account, literally says, 'For you would never commit yourself to a greater degree [a fossilised instrumental], if you wished to lie'. This translation assumes that *will* here represents *wald* (and the reported form may well be influenced by *weill* in the following line). Alternatively, one might consider Lupack's translation 'For you will never give more (than you will tomorrow, in immediate response both to the season and to Rauf's own hospitality)'. Lupack does acknowledge difficulty in accommodating the second line to this translation, but he notes that reading *nane lesing* would render that line a simple asseveration, 'that's no lie'.

310 *To mak ane lesing*: The stanza break confronts guileless collier with plausibly deceptive king; cf. *lelely* 311, or *I tell the plane* 315. But one might equally note also Rauf's use of *preif* (or *encheif*) to describe his errand, that it is like a chivalric quest and the fulfilment of a knightly vow (*cunnand*), an assertion repeated up to his climactic invocation of fate in 377.

315 *said*: Reading *hecht* would accord more closely with usual alliterative usage, and would establish a contrasting echo with 380 and 409.

316 *enchaip*: Appears in *DOST* as a unique usage.

317 *he*: i.e., Rauf, really serving as a speech-identification to his preceding one-line assent.

319 *maid*: This is another 'double-dipped' b-verse, and the disyllabic *cunnand* at its centre renders the reported text particularly recalcitrant, e.g., resistant to any obvious contracted readings. I have chosen to read the absolute *made* 'agreed'; cf. *DOST made* pp. and pp.adj., esp. sense 2 'appointed' (and with a wider range of use in OSc than ME, where the sense is normally 'manufactured, constructed').

338 Since it includes *was*, the b-verse must refer to Roland (and have his name in the preceding line as antecedent).

340 *knicht*: Singular for plural to provide the rhyme.

342 *and the*: This b-verse is again one syllable short of a metrical half-line. The dropped *the* represents a case of dissimilation in the transmission, a copyist or compositor choosing not to repeat the word after a use earlier in the line.

345 *Preichand*: The verb must have a rather broad sense, like 'exhorting' (here contextually 'reminding'). The company are literally singing a church anthem appropriate to the Advent season, a time of prophecy (as well as of penance), to be fulfilled in the miraculous birth. One might compare the insistence upon waiting for what has been promised and expecting fulfilment on the morrow in the opening of matins for Christmas Eve (York Use): 'Introit: Prestolantes redemptorem, leuate capita vestra, quoniam prope est redemptio vestra. Psalmus [94]: Venite... Versus: Hodie scietis quia veniet Dominus. Responsio: Et mane videbitis gloriam eius' ('The introit: In expectation of the redeemer, lift up your heads, for your salvation is near at hand. Psalm 94: Come. The verse: Today you will recognise that the Lord will come. The response: And in the morning you will see his majesty.'). A little later in the service, after the second lection, comes the response, 'Constantes estote; videbitis auxilium Domini super vos. Iudea et Hierusalem, nolite timere; cras egrediemini, et Dominus erit vobiscum', along with the repeated, 'Crastina die delebitur iniquitas terre, et regnabit super nos saluator mundi' ('Be firm; you will see the Lord's aid for you. Judea and Jerusalem, do not fear; tomorrow you will pass forth, and the Lord will be with you. ... Tomorrow the world's evil will be wiped out, and the saviour of the world will reign over us.').

356 *Mony wicht wyfis sone*: Walsh aptly connects the phrase with Whiting M719.

357 *ane and twentie dayis*: An unmarked accusative of (extent of) time, 'during the three weeks it lasted'. Contrast repeated *the morne*, an unmarked dative of time (at which).

363 *dew* (and cf. 383 *dawin*): This historically weak verb shows strong forms on the analogy of OE *dragan* and *cnāwan*. This past tense form also appears at *Golagros* 603.

367 *ȝone*: A metrical b-verse requires stressing this demonstrative.

370 *ȝhe*: As transmitted, the off-verse has proved problematic to editors, since it seems to require a negative – Charles was indeed alone. I think the easier solution is to see *he* as a misrepresentation of *ȝhe* 'you two', the compositor having dropped the first letter. Had this been a situation allowing for single combat, not a household scuffle, Gill thinks Charles would have retaliated. As the subsequent encounter with Roland shows, her intelligent reservations are misplaced, yet she equally rises to an inherently chivalric oath of her own in 374.

381 *gawin*: The form is presented as unique in *DOST*, although it is simply a variant of (the still unusual) *gain* n. (and cf. *MED gein* n.), all derivatives of ON *gegn* (here through the alternate form *gagn*).

386 *cantlie*: Presented in *DOST* as another unique usage, but see *MED cantli* adv., with five northern ME uses.

392 *That neuer wald set him on assay withoutin his assent*: As many past accounts, perhaps most notably Smyser 147 n.2, have noted, the poem's Roland is a rather unusual figure. Here, he is certainly restive at having to miss the Christmas Day celebration on an apparent fool's errand (a trait Charles has presumably counted upon in arranging his trick). But on the whole, this Roland lacks the *preux* rigidity often typifying his *chanson de geste* original.

395 *leid*: Given the poet's general avoidance of commonplace alliterative synonyms for 'man, warrior', the word likely reflects the other derivative of OE *lēod* (usually OE plural *lēode*), 'people, folks'. Although *DOST* distinguishes its *lede* n.2, senses 1 and 2, on the basis of overt plural marking of the noun, note *thame* 396.

400–1 The word-order is a bit convoluted, probably in order to accommodate the rhymes; translate: ‘So that I may see him in this hall before noon today’.

411 *He*: Mis-set, anticipating *saw*, as *Ha*.

415 *huit*: The form is cited as unique in *DOST huve* v. But it probably reflects haplography for the well-attested *hu[u]it*, particularly given the possibility of compositorial dissimilation from the subsequent *houerit*.

419 *followit to*: Simply the normal idiom, the preposition not translatable in modern English; see *DOST follow* v., sense 1.

420 *at bidding full bane*: Grammatically, the half-line is functionally (and provocatively) ambiguous. Does it modify the on-verse and refer to Roland’s activity? Or might one place a full stop at the cesura and join the half-line with *He* (= Rauf) at the head of the subsequent verse? One would then translate ‘(when addressed), the collier knelt obediently and courteously’.

427 *ma*: Since this form refers specifically to quantities, implicitly ‘no more people than you’.

428 Off-verse metricality depends upon the elision ‘ne’er’. For the sense of *nyse* ‘proud’, re-enforced by *comounis* 429 and *mony better than I* 430, see *DOST nice* adj., sense 3a.

434 *art*: Rather prosy, and perhaps a compositorial insertion.

435 Translate the b-verse: ‘whatever we may have (previously) pledged to do’; in this second usage, *be* is the subjunctive. However, exactly what this is to mean remains opaque to me. Roland’s fealty to Charles renders the king’s command an obligation, and one he was loath to undertake on a festival day. But he has no way of knowing Rauf to be similarly bound (and certainly does not know they are contracted to the same person), although he might assume so, given the festival day. In any event, he inadvertently acknowledges what Rauf himself believes, that the pair are equally bound by obligations potentially legible as chivalric contracts (cf. 310n).

441 *mad*: I mark in the glossary the potential ambiguity of the form, which may well represent *mait*. For other examples of *-d*/*-t* alternation, see the Introduction, p. 9. This form, potentially referring to Rauf as someone whose profession demands hard work, finds some confirmation in the *myster* of the following line.

445 *governing*: Neither *DOST governing* n. nor *govern(e)* v. recognises the sense 'livelihood', and the line appears as a unique usage at *OED governing* n. The word potentially, of course, redefines a business customarily assigned to and pursued by the *maisterfull men* of 442.

455 *grauit in gold and gowlis in grene*: Confusingly enough, the parallelism involves both the heraldic or and gules, as well as both phrases introduced by *in*; for a comparable, yet more directly stated, locution, see *Golagros* 478. In spite of *DOST grene* n., there is no vert here; the rhyme-word, as also at 666, represents *MED grain* n., sense 6 'a scarlet dye'.

457 *Ane tyger ticht to ane tre*: Papworth 57 shows that the most usual tiger in British arms relies on the presentation in *Physiologus* (cf. *Bestiary* 28–29), a tiger staring into a mirror. This depicts the ferocious and speedy beast partially tamed – the mother tiger pursuing someone who has stolen a cub and momentarily distracted in her chase by her soft maternal instinct. Knights who bear this charge thus allege, not so unlike Rauf in his rebukes of Charlemagne, their viciousness to those outside the bloodline, yet lovingness to kin. In contrast, there is nothing 'soft' about Roland's pinioned beast, which resembles but a single blazon Papworth describes, with a tiger 'collared and chained'. One might compare the famous 'bear and ragged staff' borne by the Beauchamp earls of Warwick, another instance of a blazon presenting raw ferocity held in check. The *takin of tene* is proverbial; see Whiting T284–90 (1951, 140–41, s.v. Tiger).

458 *that teneful*: i.e., Roland. As customarily, the blazon stands as a mark of chivalric identity. The b-verse is metrical, since the participial suffix *-and* represents disyllabic ON *-andi*; cf. 681 *closand*.

462 *burneist*: Since the spelling cloaks tri-syllabic *burnishit*, this is a metrical b-verse. It is, however, parenthetical, an intrusion into the ongoing sense, since the subsequent lines describe the jewelled ornament at the edges introduced by *bordourit*.

466 *reulit*: Although this verb to describe decoration occurs on three subsequent occasions (669, 670, 685), I am deeply suspicious of these readings. *DOST* presents these examples at *reul(e)* v., senses 11b and c, but all the parallels alleged there might arguably be associated with other well-attested senses of the verb. Further, in at least one use, *reulit about in reuall* 679, one might suspect possible compositorial attraction to subsequent materials. More plausible in all these instances would be *DOST raillit* pp., with roughly the same sense as that ascribed *reulit* in *DOST*, but recorded only once elsewhere in Scots, at *Howlat* 674. Cf. also the reported *inrold* of *Howlat* 344 and the note to that line (Holland 2014, 112), and *MED railen* v.1.

469 *graipis*: *DOST* presents the noun as unparalleled (and undefined). But the sense is reasonably clear, the word an Ablaut variant related to *grip* 'fastening' (from the stem, OE *grīpan*). The line is directly parallel with 467 and to be read as if 'And his greis picht with greit graipis...'.

473 *thopas*: A Northern-Scots apocopated plural after a sibilant, analogous to the familiar plural *hors*, e.g., at 813 and 817. The compositor may have been misled by the apparent singular into rendering the later *trewluuis* as singular also.

at anis: Probably a fully alliterated line rhyming aa|aa, with slant-alliteration on /t/, i.e., *a-t'anis*.

474 *iewellis*: Amours was first to suggest that the compositor's *tewellis* was an error dependent on attraction to the alliterative rhyme. The word *tool* as a term for military equipment is restricted to what is not in evidence here, bladed weaponry (as in modern slang).

484–85 Translate: 'Were he as courageous as he is well turned out (presumably referring both to Roland's potential for athleticism, as well as his flashy armour, cf. 550–51, 558), the man who (= *He* 485) dared endure a hostile encounter with him would indeed be mighty'. Although perhaps a bit overawed, Rauf will accept the dare and inadvertently show himself what he does not quite believe he is, 'michtie'.

489 *vndertuk* (*vndertak* L): A small bit of mis-set type; cf. 529.

494 Translate: 'until the sun has reached its midday apex'.

501 *as I am command*: This half-line follows directly from line 500a, *as* here functionally having the force of 'since'.

506 *sechand*: Translate: 'You found me seeking nothing that was in accord with having a hostile intent'. A variety of editors, including Beattie, accommodate the word to the alliterative pattern and read *fettand.* For a general comment on this impulse (the line has adequate alliteration, rhyming ax|aa), see pp. 21–22 above. One might also notice that *fettand* 'bearing with me' is in fact inapposite; like any prudent man on the roads, Rauf is armed, if to Roland derisively so (cf. 515–18).

519 *It is lyke sayd*: Hazlitt emended to *This lyked* 'This amused', but such a reading ignores the force of *lyke...That.*

520 *stubill*: *DOST* offers but a single analogous use, in a variant reading at Henryson, *Moral Fables* 253, 'In stubbill array' (tentatively glossed in Fox's note 'in an awkward condition'). A metrical b-verse probably requires an inflected infinitive, either *stryken* or *strykë*.

522 *vnburelie*: Following *DOST*, the word is unique to this poem, where it appears twice more, at 695 and 806. The second use is instructive, since although Rauf appears lower-class and out of his element, he is indeed a *burelie* (or as 698 has it, *stalwart*) man.

523 See Whiting F571 and T119 (1949, 174, s.v. Foul; and 1951, 139, s.v. Thing). The proverb is opposed to that in the preceding distych, and the line requires an implicit 'just as' as introduction.

532 With the b-verse, cf. Whiting B456 (1949, 138, s.v. Bell 4).

534 *anhertance*: Editors have universally accepted the printed text, *aduertance*, although it is a word and sense unnoted in either *DOST* or *MED*. The compositor is attempting to reproduce some form of *DOST anherdance* n. (and cf. *anherd* v. and *enherd* v.). I've performed a minimal correction, in effect taking the reported form as an example of turned type and misinterpretation of the ascender of *h* as if *d*.

535 Translate: 'I've no reason to feel frustrated about my quest'. The line rhymes xaa|ax, with the third stave provided by slant alliteration, *n'errand*.

537 *Bot gif*: The off-verse is reasonably pellucid: by going on his covenanted trip to find 'Wymond', Rauf will fulfil Rolland's *cunnand* as well. This material follows grammatically from line 536b. But the dependant clause of the on-verse has proved remarkably opaque; cf. Amours's note and Putter 156 n.28.

This is an at least partially soluble problem. *Bot gif* would follow fairly naturally from line 535, rather than introducing material in any direct relationship with the remainder of line 537: 'I should not need feel frustrated, unless...'. Meanwhile, however confusingly, the b-verse follows from line 536. As subsequent notes will indicate, syntactic difficulties like this (and longlines split in accord with various relationships with their surround) mark the later interchange between Roland and Magog.

However, exactly how this on-verse shows a condition Roland would find 'noyful' is not so clear. Here the problem is *forrow*, normally a preposition 'before' and at least sensible in its phrase (*forrow now* = 'before this time'), but not in the overall construction. If *forrow* is indeed a preposition, there must be a missing adjective, if alliterating, something like *faynt* 'deceitful' or *fraward* 'disobedient'. The alternative is to consider an (unrecorded) adjectival sense for *forrow*, 'eager (to go away)': 'I wouldn't need feel frustrated, unless I had found you...'. There are the additional problems that *But gif* may have been attracted to this line on the basis of the use two lines hence and that *forrow now* potentially represents some form of compositorial dittography.

Any active correction of the verse being purely hypothetical, I think the best I can do is lay out some alternatives.

538b Translate, 'don't believe that I mean anything different'; cf. 560.

545 Cf. Putter's translation (156 n.29): 'I don't need to fulfil my errand any earlier than noon'. First, one should note that the line is implicitly (or so taken by Rauf) an injunction to haste, yet its relationship to the preceding line is rather fuzzy – as it stands, a relatively senseless cause of result. (It is possible that the compositor has set *sen* for adverbial *syne*, and the clauses independent.) Further, like Riddy's rendition of line 31, Putter reproduces what the line should say, but not what the reported text does. As transmitted, the line lacks any word implying completion, although that is plainly the issue; one might suggest reading *neich* 'approach (the end of?)' or assume compositorial haplography through an editorial insertion like *myne erand [ende]*. But again, as in my previous notes, this seems a situation where one might best only lay out alternatives.

550 *hew*: Probably *DOST hew* n.2, recorded only twice, as potentially a word separate from the common noun 'colour', in records of 1511–12 and 1530. *DOST* offers no definition, but contextually the word refers to 'stuf', material to go into garments or adorn a saddle.

551 *bone*: The adjective is recorded only three times in *DOST*, and this phrase, presumably a calque on French *(de) bonne foi* 'sincerity', is unparalleled. Translate the line: 'You'll be shown as weak in your ability to uphold your vow/word', i.e., to back up in combat that overbearing language (for Roland a sworn obligation) to which Rauf feels he has been subjected. The connection with French idiom may imply that Rauf, just as in his earlier querulous assessment of Roland's flashiness, may intend the locution as ironic – flighty French court-stuff, not plain Scots.

559 *all*: If one assumes that metrical stress and alliteration coincide in this line (rhyming ab|ba), a metrical b-verse depends on construing this word as a plural adjective (modifying *weidis*), rather than the adverb 'completely'.

561 Cf. Whiting B466 (1949, 143, s.v. Born).

562 *band*: As Beattie, among others, suggested, the word has been mis-set (dittography involving two similarly formed graphemes with ascenders).

578 The line modifies *wy* in the preceding.

600 *furth gat*: The transmitted b-verse is unmetrical, with only two monosyllabic dips. I have repaired it by inverting the received word-order; other options, for example, reading *[full] glaid*, are certainly possible. In support of this second option, one might adduce haplography following a word also beginning *fu-*.

604 *Bot*: *Bo* is a simple misprint.

beget: Presented as a unique form in *DOST*. As Amours pointed out, this spelling represents the verb *bege(c)k*, which does not appear in *DOST* but the later *SND*. But this is, in a culture given to creative invective, the sort of slang that often passes beneath written notice. There is a hint that the root was current at a point roughly contemporary with *Rauf* in Dunbar, 'Fastern's evin in hell' 29 'all... lewche and maid gekkis' (*DOST gek* n. 'a derisive gesture, mockery, a trick'). On the other hand, at Dunbar's 'Twa Mariit Wemen' 452, 'With gret engyne to bejaip ther jolyus husbandis', the alliteration shows that the Maitland Folio's variant 'to begaik' is a late sixteenth-century scribalism, reflecting a spate of uses just following *Rauf*'s publication (mainly from the 1580s).

Amours's further suggestion that the rhyming *ȝet* 607 could read *hek* 'hatch' seems to me less perspicacious. For this and similar assonant rhymes, in which any unvoiced stop may rhyme with any other, see the Introduction, p. 9. The compositors, who set a reasonably commonplace verb for one they plainly did not understand, are more apt to have been guided to their reading by the rhyme-word, than offering the pair of substitutions required in Amours's more complicated scenario.

609 *gedling*: *DOST* identifies the noun (and its further appearance at 618) as unique. Translate: 'where are you going so quickly?'

610 *ane gift heir I geif*: Amours translates 'I have something to say', and following him, some editors (e.g., Browne and Walsh) directly gloss *gift* as 'news'. Unfortunately, *DOST* provides no citation for such a sense. Cf. however, *OED give* v., sense 8 (and see sense 21) for a usage recorded in ME from *c*. 1300; the clause essentially parallels the following on-verse: 'I swear to you, I assure you'.

615 *Gif*: The compositor's *Git* has been attracted to following *t*-.

628 *Vnbraissit*: I follow Browne's suggestion, supported by *DOST*.

636 *swet*: Glosses like Riddy's 'sweated', although in accord with the more elegant *DOST swete* v., sense 4 ('toiled') are only comical. This word, in conjunction with *seruice*, probably represents *sewit*, a form of *DOST sew(e)* v, senses 3 and 4.

640 *thame*: The plural rather loosely follows from *all* in the preceding line, contextually both Rauf's *capill* and his *laid*.

641 *in hy he haikit*: Cf. Henryson, *Moral Fables* 919, 'in haist haikit'. Given the root sense of the verb, 'to trudge, go laboriously', the clause presumably means something like 'He went on so quickly that he almost stumbled'.

648 As Browne first suggested, *He trowit* at the head of the line is surely a compositorial insertion. It has been induced by the line's delaying the actual verb to rhyming position.

651 Translate: 'They accounted Rauf as worth almost none of their attention'. Literally, the syntax runs 'They accounted

Rauf in their attention as almost nothing'; *not... almaist* are construed together, and the first of these words, as sporadically in the text, has been written for more explicit *nocht*.

652 Translate: 'He saw that neither acting humbly nor moderately might improve things there'; the following line gives the result of this perception.

656 *threit*: I simply correct the transmitted plural *thretis*; *with threit* probably represents an adverbial qualifier, rather than, as the compositor apparently assumed, a statement of literal action(s).

663 *apperrellit*: Like all editors, I correct the compositor's misperception of their exemplar.

668 *flamand ferly*: Following on the reference to the royal fleurs-de-lys in the preceding line, this must refer to the oriflamme, the red banner traditionally borne by kings of France. This has three pointed ends and a golden sun with flame-like beams. It appears, for example, in *Chanson de Roland* 3093–95.

669 *reuall of reid*: Smyser 149, elaborating upon Browne's note, suggests that this decoration, particularly in association with *flour-de-lycis*, recalls the Scots royal arms, with its 'double tressour, flory'. For a more meticulous description, see *Howlat* 365–77 and 365–66nn (Holland 2014, 113). Both Browne and Smyser point to (legendary) Scottish alliances with Charlemagne, offered as historical precursors to 'the auld alliance'; in these accounts, the allied king was extended a heraldic privilege otherwise reserved for Scottish royalty. As the preceding note would imply, such a heraldic identification is quite plausible, but equally, given the wheel of the stanza, the decoration described might represent a vine-stem bearing a range of flowers.

674 *dosour*: *DOST* provides but a single parallel, Henryson, *Moral Fables* 336, 'Betwix the dosor and the wall scho ['the rurall mous'] crap'. But cf. a variant version of *Awntyrs* 444, where the word occurs conjoined with the *bancouris* of line

682, as well as analogous juxtapositions (especially in legal records) cited in *MED doser* n., sense 1.

677 *thir*: Riddy responds to the clearly erroneous *he* by combining it with the previous word to produce *seinye*; she reads the phrase *in seinye* 'as an emblem' (of what?). In spite of Riddy's demurer, I find *in seir*, even in the absence of direct parallels, reasonably sensible as an adverbial phrase 'variously', although the form may represent original *in fere* ('all together'), attracted to the line's alliterative stave. I perform the minimal surgery of bringing transmitted *he* into accord with its plural antecedent, *dosouris*.

680 *carpitit*: While there is no problem about the sense conveyed, and *carpit* might represent some variety of contracted pp., I think it more responsible to see the transmitted form as haplographic.

681 *quemely*: Another lexical item presented as unique to the poem in *DOST*. *MED quemeli* adv. is similarly of restricted use (three citations).

683 *Greit squechonis on hicht*: The best-known British examples of such decoration appear in English royal chapels, rather than palace halls, e.g., the plaques of the Garter knights in St George's chapel at Windsor Castle. Perhaps more relevant might be the polychromed stone armorials once in the cornices at St Stephen's chapel, Westminster; see Tristram 48–54, 57–58, 206–19, and plates 1–6; Smith 232–50.

689 The b-verse has an implicit verb of motion.

691 *anis*: Probably the rhyme-driven form for *ane*, i.e., 'him alone' or 'him only'.

701 *formest ... in feir*: 'The most prominent in the company'; cf. the slightly varied form, also referring to Charles, at 578.

706 The line apparently completes a comparative construction begun in the missing one that preceded.

708 Presumably requiring an implicit verb of motion, e.g., 'into coming'.

709 *sair*: Ambiguously might modify either *dreid* or *begylit*.

718 Translate the b-verse, 'I must have been possessed (to wish to)'. *say* in the following line implies that Rauf wishes he could say this as extenuation for inappropriate behaviour. His plan for one kind of *chaiping* (cf. 316) has been transformed a different form of *chaip*. Translate 719b–22, '... before I trade here. If I can escape from these circumstances that have left me feeling discomfited, no man, however wise he were, would...'. Of course, the surprise is that, although a transformation of sorts will occur, it will not be initially of Rauf's *cheir*, but from *carll* to *knicht* (cf. line 745).

728 *grome*: The alliterative synonym *gome* might seem attractive, but Scots routinely uses the transmitted form to describe lordly men, e.g., persistently in *Golagros* (first at 148).

730 *ford*: Amours persuasively identified the form with *ford* 'way'. The off-verse parallels *frostit...sa fell*, and *war* is the verb of both members; translate, 'The frosts were so fierce, and the way so constrained'. The alternative editorial suggestion, construing *ford* as 'for it', seems to me senseless.

733–37 The wheel communicates, 'If only we could start this all over again (I'd have behaved differently)'. *Or ony knicht* 736 is parallel to *thyself* 733.

742 *forbot*: *DOST* offers a single analogous use of the word, Rolland's *Seven Sages* 1586. Translate the off-verse, '(that) such a behaviour should be my thanks...' (*war* here is subjunctive).

743 *ill*: The metre requires a monosyllable. In the print, OSc *ill* survives only when necessary for the rhyme (39, 108) and has otherwise been replaced by *euill*. Unlike many of my corrections, where syllabic adjustments represent merely variant spellings, this is a substantive error and requires explicit textual marking.

744 *Hym semis*: This locution is equivalent to the more straightforward *He semis* (cf. 753); see *DOST seme* v., sense 6c.

745 *for*: The preposition carries just a hint of amused ambiguity: is it the expected 'because of' (*DOST*'s sense 1) or the qualified 'in spite of' (sense 6)? Certainly, the following wheel implies that stalwartness, however gruff, might be a sufficient qualification for Rauf's commendation.

749 *That*: Although *þā þā* 'those who' might have been idiomatic OE in such a context, the compositor has probably set the previous word twice.

752 This line specifies the *mony worthie* of the preceding.

753 *se for*: cf. *DOST se* v., senses 15b (*se for* = 'take heed to, see to') or 19 (*se to* = 'take care about'). Although, as subsequent lines indicate, Rauf is plainly *wicht*, the *ordour* he now enters might require additional discipline.

757 *ressonabill richt*: This legalism, most narrowly 'clear title' or 'defensible ownership of a property', reverberates through thirteen-line poems. Examples occur at *Awntyrs* 350 and 362, *Howlat* 968, and *Golagros* 189 (with later partial analogues). One hopes that a former Oxford D.Phil. student, Jennifer Reuer, will some day complete her intensive research into the topic. Rather broadly, the phrase appears to differentiate tyrannous lordship, indifferent to the *richt* of others, from proper behaviour. Here the allusion is inflected by the persistent appeal to 'ressoun' or 'skill' (or more broadly, 'suith') that underpins Rauf's proverbialism; see Introduction, pp. 19–20. One might note that line 760 extends to Rauf a heritable, not personal 'right', a permanent social elevation to his line.

764 *worthy*: Punctuation necessarily disambiguates: is Charles referring to 'my honourable will' or to an 'honour' only potential, that Rauf will achieve in battle? As the poem's narrative develops, any squeamishness that Charles expresses will be promptly undone when Rauf encounters Magog; cf. 789.

thy schone that thow wan: Although not apparently recognised in *DOST*, the usual medieval locution; cf. *OED shoe* n., sense 2i, and *MED sho* n., sense 1c. 'Winning one's spurs' through combat is probably a distinctively modern notion; in the Middle Ages, spurs formed an inherent property of knighthood, as at *Piers Plowman* B 18.12–14 (and cf. 811 below).

766 *ken*: On the rhyme with *man*, see the Introduction, pp. 9–10.

772 The line follows directly from, and expands upon *with armour* 770. Similarly *Sextie squyaris of fee* 773, an endowment analogous to the armoury, depends on *gart richt* 770.

779 *hecht*: The construction is completed by *To* in the following line. The ennobled Rauf immediately begins to 'talk alliteratively'.

784 *liddernes*: Presented in *DOST* as a unique usage. The distych, of course, echoes Roland's response to Charles's 'tough love' at 598–99.

797 *hecht* (similarly *fecht* 874): For these rhymes, see the Introduction, p. 10 n.14.

798 *that he had thair bene*: i.e., previously, when he first met Roland. Analogously, *than first* 809 refers to the disparity between the glittering Roland of the previous encounter and the ostensibly savage figure Rauf now sees. The confusion of identities is further underscored when Rauf's *bid[ing] be the bair way* is echoed when Magog *semit baldly to abyde* 805, as if expecting a contest.

803 *cameill*: Of course, one expects from analogous Charlemagne materials (see Introduction pp. 11–13), that the outlandish mount introduces a Hispano-Moorish 'Saracen'. Yet traditional English pubs called 'The Saracen's Head' in less enlightened times displayed a black man, a sign of double marginalisation, emphasising not simply credal, but racial differences. Such representations, just as here, blur these differences into a general 'otherness'.

Here the most pregnant detail is perhaps the last, the 'Saracen's' name, 913 *Magog*. This is biblically derived; cf. Gen 10:12, Ez 38:2 and most prominently Apoc 20:7–8. In addition to these sources, the name appears as commander of a barbarous army shut out from the west in Alexander romances (e.g., the ME *Wars of Alexander* 5609–28, or the 'defective' *Mandeville's Travels* ch. 21). Although *Mandeville* associates them with the ten lost tribes of Israel, these forces presumably represent the proverbially 'barbarous Scythians' – and significantly for further detail here, *Wars* describes these as 'of þire Tartaryns...kyngs'.

Equally, Apoc 20:7–8 associates Gog and Magog's armies with Antichrist's persecution of the church, a prominent sign of the end-time. There is a typically encyclopaedic discussion at *Prick of Conscience* 4449–90, explicated with further references in Wood's excellent notes (Morris 2013, 326–27); see further Anderson (and Barry's detailed review) for further materials on these legends. But, as for example in Geoffrey of Monmouth's identification of 'Goemagog' as a native giant to be destroyed so that Brutus may settle Britain (*Historia* 1.21), the name would seem to identify, not a Muslim, but simply a powerful and tyrannous exotic.

Other elements of the account would suggest a similar blurriness in the depiction. For the repeated descriptor, *Sarazine*, see the careful (and profuse) *MED Sarasin* adj. and n.1 (cf. *DOST Saracene* n. and adj.). From the oldest English citations, the term is not marked as 'Muslim', but rather 'pagan, unbeliever'; indeed, in traditional Arthurian materials, it refers to the as yet unbaptised fifth- and sixth-century Anglo-Saxon invaders.

Similarly, 849 *Mahoun* accords in sense with that other derivative from the prophet's name, *mawmet*. It means simply 'idolatrer' or the name of an idolatrer's deity. (It is singularly inappropriate as a slur, given the greater resistance to representation in Islam than even traditional Judaism – as inept as attempting to insult adherents of either religion by calling them 'pig-eaters'). At the best, this term, along with *Termagant*, should be seen as meaning 'following a false god' – and not necessarily Allah – rather than anything more narrowly definitional.

Here mystery play usage is telling. In the Wakefield cycle, the Egyptian Pharaoh, the Roman Caesar Augustus, and the Idumean Herod the Great are all characterised by this devotion. The York cycle is more restrained: its Caiphas (play 29), sees Jesus as a follower of 'Mahoun' (thus, 'heretic [as regards Judaic Temple practice]'?), and its besotted Herod (play 31) persistently swears 'by the bloode that Mahoun bledde' (a joke, that he is incapable of his own religious practice, but assimilates it to Christian 'myth'?). All these figures share with later invocations of 'the termagant' and with the poem's Magog a penchant for rodomontade, part of their presentation as self-serving tyrants. Cf. the, in this context predictable, 'succudrously' 855 and Roland's charge in line 908 'Ʒe Sarazeins ar succuderus and self-willit ay'.

Given this sort of background, it is perhaps no surprise to find 903 *Chane of Tartarie*, properly a reference to the Mongols and their Yuan dynasty. Such an identification can scarcely be perceived as entirely negative. Texts like the travels of Marco Polo and Fr Odoric of Pordenone (both extensively recorded in fifteenth-century Britain), as well as their local derivative 'Mandeville', found much to praise in China. Kubilai Khan's court at Shangdu (Xanadu) forms an overwhelming climax of regal civility in the last mentioned of these texts. These accounts were originally driven by a desire for possible Mongol conversion, an effort to utilise this horde as a potential ally, a fifth column at the rear, *against* Islam. For some relatively recent studies of Sino-European contact, Silk Road cultural interchanges, see Crossley.

Thus, to return to line 803's *cameill*: uses elsewhere simply point to a mount appropriate to '(dangerous and overbearing) aliens', but, from our perspective, recalcitrantly diverse in their originary force. Cf., for example, the camel-riding Jews of *The Siege of Jerusalem* 452–60, 573–81; or those of Roman allies at *Morte Arthure* 2282–89. One might also recall Chaucer's Clerk, denigrating yet another group to be marginalised, mouthy women, 'Syn ye be strong as is a greet camaille' (*Canterbury Tales* IV.1196). Notice that in *Rauf* the camel promptly morphs into a *blonk*, perhaps to be neutrally glossed 'mount'.

809 Following from the association of *first* with Rauf's initial encounter with and vow to Roland (see 798n), *he*[1] refers to Magog, but *he*[2] to Rauf, who is then the subject in the following line. But of course, adding to the confusion, the line might be equally applicable to Rauf, in his newly bestowed armour a good deal more threatening than he had been before.

810 *foundis*: Amours suggested reading *faindis* 'attempts' (which would represent compositorial dissimilation after *fand* in the preceding rhyme). But such an adjustment still does not account for the rhyme-word *se*, and I find Riddy's suggestion, essentially that this means 'render visible (by unhelming him)' rather limp.

Neither editor quite registers that this line is but one of a set, 807–11, that describes a charge, for which the verb *founden* might well be appropriate. Moreover, there is a further contextual signal, also overlooked. The poem has passed into emphatic alliterative mode for a traditional alliterative subject, a battle scene, and the stanza stresses the point by couplet alliteration. (Although 808b breaks this pattern, that half-line is bound to what follows by introducing the rhyme-sound of the following couplet.) The general sense appears, 'He advances, so that he might [???] him through his power', and the obvious rhyme-word is *fe*, not *se* (perhaps attracted from 804?). This is not a reading easy to defend, since the verb generally means 'hire for a task' (although that might well be relevant to a formerly commercially engaged collier). But I would think that might suggest a sense like 'pay him out' (an ambiguity present in ME *hiren*, which means both 'contract labour' and 'stipulate "hire"', a wage for the work). Once again, rather than change the text, I explore possibilities.

forcenes: Another lexical item presented as unique in *DOST* (again at 816). But cf. Gawain 646, *DOST forcy* adj. and *MED forci* adj.

821 *Bait*: Editors have read the form in the print variously: Tonndorf as *Baft*, Herrtage as *Bair*. I think Walsh's *Bait* (ambiguous, representing either OE *bāt* or a back-spelling for OE *bēot*) probably correct. The b-verse here is an appendage of that in the preceding line.

823 *To tyne*: Parallel to *to leif* in the preceding line, and like it, dependent upon *laith*; translate, 'They were reluctant to stop (and thereby) to lose'.

824 *vincussing*: The noun customarily, as Amours saw, means 'victory' (*DOST* cites only four uses). It here must have an unparalleled passive sense, not conquering but being conquered.

830 *heid*: Perhaps, given the subsequent line 837, for *heit* 'heat'.

836 *ȝarne*: Most editors construe this form as a verb and the half-line as direct speech, 'Long to yield', i.e., 'give up'. My sense of alliterative usage (and of direct speech in combat situations) suggests it is rather the adverb; translate, 'Each party calls out eagerly for the other to surrender'.

837 *and tak mair of the licht*: Unless *tak* is stressed, this half-line is double-dipped; further, *of the* appears potentially otiose. But I have no idea what this might be supposed to be saying. In conjunction with raising his visor, it may simply mean that Rauf 'let the light chill his sweaty brow'. But it may be some version of a common set-phrase, e.g., *DOST licht* n.1, sense 1b, *be in another's licht* or *sit in one's licht* 'be obstructed by someone else'; or sense 5f, *bring* (or *cum*, *pas*, *go*) *to licht* 'become visible, make manifest or known' – and thus mean something like '(He withdrew) and could look about, as well as become visible'.

842 *repreif*: A metrical b-verse requires an inflected disyllabic form. These first four lines are addressed, as the subsequent reply indicates, to Magog, whom Rauf has confused with Roland. The agreement (see 561–65) was that they should fight singly, whereas Rauf believes 'the fake Roland', the Saracen, to have deliberately arranged to set an ally on him.

849 *Mahoun or Termagant*: See 803n above.

853–54 The comic ending of reconciliation demands that, for all his attention to covenanted or contracted behaviour, Rauf will implicitly be required to violate his initial chivalric vow.

856 Translate the line, 'I will have no pleasure, should I allow you (to live on) amicably (i.e., without further fighting)'. But one might suggest that the compositor should have set *leit*; translate this version, 'I will have no pleasure in life, should I abandon you amicably'.

857 *He*: i.e., Magog, who strikes Rauf, *the kene knicht* 859. Although momentarily stunned, Rauf in his turn recovers to strike a counter-blow, *ruschit vp agane* 861.

871 *that*: 'Who', so that the off-verse follows directly from *Sarazine* 870: 'a Saracen, who battles so fiercely in order to destroy our Christian men'.

875 *weill*: In all ME textual traditions, alternation between this empty intensifier and the equally vapid *full* is positively endemic. Here the latter would add a rhyming stave ('completely evident').

881 *breif*: *DOST* cites the verb form as unique and suggests it is connected with *brethe* n.1 'anger'. Browne wished to emend to *Bray* 'frighten'. Both are troubled by the fact that the Scots verb *breve* always refers to written materials. But *MED breven* v. is scarcely so limited, particularly not in alliterative contexts (e.g., 'Breue me, bryȝt', *Pearl* 755). Translate, 'Don't speak to me so pridefully'. The 'surquidous Saracen' takes on a task that Rauf has judged unfair, to combat a pair.

883 One detail rather unnoted in discussions of the slightly subheroic Roland of the poem: it is conventional in the pseudo-Turpin chronicle and its derivatives for the Christian knight to urge conversion on a Muslim opponent. But customarily he is equally pleading for the cessation of his own martial acts, not as surrogate for an actual combatant. In this poem, Rauf has subsumed his martial position.

884–87 Although I don't mark the text, I would strongly suspect that the transmitted lines 884 and 886 have been transposed. In the repetitive form of the thirteen-line stanza, mistakes like this are easy enough to make, and scribes or compositors looking for the next rhyme-word are apt, unless careful, to come up with the wrong one. Potentially, one such error has occurred previously, at 134, and cf. the Asloan MS at *Howlat* 370–71, among other examples. Here the transposition of materials indicates that the compositor caught himself in time to ensure that no text was lost, but was not quite honest enough to insert omitted materials in the proper place, instead just setting the omitted line out of order. I would suggest reading:

'Na', said Schir Rolland, 'that war na resoun,
For that war na wassalage, sum men wald say.
The tane is in power to mak that presoun.
I trow in the mekle God that maist of michtis may;
I rid that thow hartfully forsaik thy Mahoun.

Thus, one avoids the slightly confusing transition in the transmitted lines 884–85, which might suggest that 'the mekel God' is 'The tane' who could imprison any Saracen; correspondingly, the power that God might bestow on the single Christian warrior leads somewhat more naturally to Roland's appeal for conversion.

885 *that*: One should probably simply read 'thee'. In the context, 'The tane...to mak that', the compositor appears to have exchanged demonstratives ('That ane...to mak the[e]').

887 *hartfully*: Modifies the non-adjacent *rid*.

891–92 The poem offers only tastes of the conventional thirteen-line stanza thematic, the concluding death lyric, again in 916–19. Note 923, which implies that worldly prosperity/governance in essence continues as heavenly.

895 Either of two translations seems probable: either 'you are only offering deference (reading 'bot') ...', or (reading 'but'), 'You are performing without deference to those who could care less'. *thame* anticipates *counsingis* 896.

896 *of my counsingis*: Modifying the nouns at the head of the following line.

897 *schame*: The noun implies either or both 'to your shame' or 'to their shame', i.e., they attacked you in order to dishonour you or that, in their onslaughts, they were shamed/defeated. The reciprocal ambiguity is to the point here (recall the repeated rhymes of the Rauf–Magog battle stanzas, or the slightly ambiguous pronouns, also a feature of the earlier Rauf–Roland meeting): rather than addressing opposites, there are slippery similarities among the combatants.

901–6 The lines rather resist any punctuation. The argument simultaneously presents both the planned despoliation and the message that threatens it, eventually settling to elaborate the latter.

903 *Chane of Tartarie*: See 803n.

904 *him*: i.e., Charlemagne, continuing from line 902. Just as Rauf's pursuit of 'Wymond' had been earlier, Magog is engaged in a disrupted messaging – and Roland engaged with someone he finds proud above his station.

907 *it seruis of nocht*: This parenthetical half-line represents *DOST serve* v.1, sense 19 'to be of use'. The valueless or useless 'it' is presumably Magog's message, identified by Roland as merely testimony to customary 'Saracen' behaviour he perceives as overweening.

908 *self-willit*: Another bit of lexis presented in *DOST* as unique. Although it records a variety of forms analogous to the compound, uses recorded in *MED*, excepting *self-wille* n., appear equally uncommon (and often confined to glossaries).

909 The line sounds as if it ought to be a proverb (another example of Roland's having absorbed Rauf's demotic). But nothing similar appears in Whiting, who has only the simile denoting speed 'Like fire of flint' (F189–90). But some of the pungency of that expression derives from the paradox, here rather inverted, that hot and flickering flame emerges from stone cold and inert.

910 *als fer as he may*: Implicitly 'so far as God allows him'.

912 Translate, 'Anyone who lies in wait to bring pain on Christians is my mate/near relation'.

913 *Magog*: See 803n.

914 Not a 'double-dipped' b-verse, since *euer* probably carries stress, but dissociated from the rhyming syllable *war*.

918 Cf. Whiting L59 (1959, 197, s.v. Land).

924–27 There are essentially two ongoing clauses, disposed in symmetrical halves of the lines. 'wyfe' 924a is developed by the appositives in the succeeding pair of on-verses, while the reason for Jane's desirability, that she is 'worthie', is elaborated in the corresponding off-verses and concluded in 927.

929 *I do the out of dispair*: Although *DOST* does not recognise the phrase or the usage, as Browne saw, this is simply a pleonastic asseveration, 'I put you out of doubt', 'I'm telling you truly'.

935 *gold*: The reading has been assimilated to the following line.

938 *that mair may*: Translate, 'who has greater power (than Mahoun)'.

948–51 The lines seem to suggest that the trio forms a kind of chivalric trinity, and line 951b must, in spite of an intervening clause, follow on 950b. In that context, 'to leif and to die | as Christ had þame kend' would seem to take on some of the ambiguity of Spenser's 'dead as liuing' (*Faerie Queene* 1.1.2.3): 'dead while alive, living once dead'.

952 The metrical rules for the off-verse require the disyllabic form *gamin*, perhaps suppressed in implicit haplography before following *an*-.

965 *he*: Given *him* 963, the most proximate independent pronoun, *he* here and in next line, especially given the repetitive appositive of 965b, must be Rauf.

966 *thame*: This little word has caused a great deal of editorial concern. Amours found the half-line problematic, eventually translated it 'to leave them in rightful possession', and still was not satisfied. Browne suggested emending to *thair*, and Riddy emended to *thane*, translating 'to live then in their estate'. But although ill-attested, *leif thame* is a respectable Scots reflexive form, 'to continue life (in a specified way, here "together *in richt*")'; see *DOST lefe* v.3, sense 2a (a), citing *The Buke of the Chess* 532.

967–69 *ane fair place... In the name of Sanct Iuly*: For hospitals dedicated to the support of wayfarers, particularly pilgrims (their primary function), see Clay (1909, 6–14); and for English dedications to St Julian, 259. For the abundant records of Scottish hospitals, see Cowan and Easson (1976, 162–209; surprisingly, they record no dedications to Julian – the nearest miss is St Giles, Edinburgh (perhaps relevant, as this saint is distinguished by a wilderness hostel and saving a stag from a royal hunt).

Bibliography

Primary Texts

The Actis and Deidis of Schir William Wallace 1570, introd. W. A. Craigie 1940. STS 3rd ser. 12. New York.

Amours, F. J., ed. 1897. *Scottish Alliterative Poems in Riming Stanzas*. 2 vols. STS 1st ser. 27, 38. Edinburgh and London.

Barber, Richard, trans. and introd. 1993. *Bestiary: being an English version of the Bodleian Library, Oxford, MS Bodley 754.* Woodbridge.

Bawcutt, Priscilla, and Felicity Riddy, eds. 1987. *Longer Scottish Poems Volume One 1375–1650*. Edinburgh. (the edition of *Rauf* by Riddy).

Child, Francis J., ed. 1883–98, rep. 2003. *The English and Scottish Popular Ballads*. 5 vols. Mineola, NY.

Craigie, William A., ed. 1923–25. *The Asloan Manuscript: A Miscellany in Prose and Verse*. 2 vols. STS ns 14, 16. Edinburgh and London.

——, ed. 1951–58. *The Poems of James VI of Scotland.* 2 vols. STS 3rd series 22, 26. Edinburgh.

Douglas, Gavin 2003. *The Shorter Poems*, ed. Priscilla Bawcutt. STS 5th ser. 2. Edinburgh.

Dunbar, William 1998. *The Poems*, ed. Priscilla Bawcutt. 2 vols. Glasgow.

Furrow, Melissa M., ed. 2013. *Ten Bourdes*. Kalamazoo, MI.

Geoffrey of Monmouth 2007. *The History of the Kings of Britain.* Ed. Michael D. Reeve; trans. Neil Wright. Woodbridge.

Hary's Wallace 1968–69. Ed. Matthew P. McDiarmid. STS 4th ser. 4–5. Edinburgh.

Hazlitt, W. Carew, rev. ed. 1895. *Early Popular Poetry of Scotland and the Northern Border*. 2 vols. London.

Herrtage, Sidney J. H., ed. 1882. *The English Charlemagne Romances. Part VI. The Taill of Rauf Coilyear*. EETS e.s. 39. London.

Holland, Richard 2014. *The Buke of the Howlat*, ed. Ralph Hanna. STS 5th ser. 12. Edinburgh.

Laing, David, ed. 1822, 1826. *Select Remains of the Ancient Popular Poetry of Scotland.* Edinburgh (for reprinted versions, see Hazlitt and Small).

Lupack, Alan, ed. 1990. *Three Middle English Charlemagne Romances.* Kalamazoo, MI.

[*Mandeville's Travels.*] 2002. *The Defective Version of Mandeville's Travels.* Ed. M. C. Seymour. EETS o.s. 319. Oxford.

Morris, Richard 2013. *Richard Morris's Prick of Conscience*, ed. Ralph Hanna and Sarah Wood. EETS o.s. 342. Oxford.

Shepherd, Stephen, ed. forthcoming. *Middle English Romances*. 2nd edn. New York.

Sir Gawain and the Carl of Carlisle, in Two Versions 1951. Ed. Auvo Kurvinen. Helsinki.

Small, John, ed. 1885. *Select Remains of the Ancient Popular and Romance Poetry of Scotland*. Edinburgh and London.

Speed, Diane, ed. 1987, rep. 1993. *Medieval English Romances*. 2 vols. 3rd edn. Durham.

Spenser, Edmund 1977. *The Faerie Queene*. Ed. A. C. Hamilton. London.

The Taill of Rauf Coilyear: A Scottish Metrical Romance of the Fifteenth Century 1903. Ed. William H. Browne. Baltimore, MD.

The Taill of Rauf Coilyear: mit literarhistorischer, grammatischer und metrischer Einleitung 1894. Ed. M. Tonndorf. Berlin.

The Taill of Rauf Coilyear printed by Robert Lekpreuik at St Andrews in 1572: a facsimile of the only known copy (Keppie Facsimilies, no. 1) 1966. Ed. William Beattie. Edinburgh.

The Tale of Ralph the Collier: An Alliterative Romance 1989. Ed. Elizabeth Walsh. New York.

Turpines Story: A Middle English Translation of the Pseudo-Turpin Chronicle 2004. Ed. Stephen Shepherd. EETS o.s. 322. Oxford.

The Wars of Alexander 1989. Ed. Hoyt N. Duggan and Thorlac Turville-Petre. EETS s.s. 10. Oxford.

Wedderburn, Robert 1979. *The Complaynt of Scotland*. Introd. A. M. Stewart. STS 4th ser. 11. Edinburgh.

Wyntoun 1903–14. *The Original Chronicle of Andrew of Wyntoun*. Ed. F. J. Amours. 6 vols. STS n.s. 50, 53, 54, 56, 57, 63. Edinburgh.

Secondary Studies

Aitken, A. J. 1997. 'The Pioneers of Anglicised Speech in Scotland'. *Scottish Language* 16, 1–36.

—— (ed. Caroline Macafee) 2002. *The Older Scots Vowels: A History of the Stressed Vowels of Older Scots from the beginnings to the Eighteenth Century.* STS 5th ser. 1. Edinburgh.

Aldis, Harry G. 1904; rep. 1970. *A List of Books Printed in Scotland before 1700: including those printed furth of the realm for Scottish booksellers, with brief notes on the printers and stationers.* Edinburgh.

Anderson, A. R. 1932. *Alexander's Gate, Gog and Magog, and the Inclosed Nations*. Cambridge, MA [and see Phillips Barry's 1933 review, *Speculum* 8, 264–70.]

Barron, W. R. J. 1982. 'Alliterative Romance and the French Tradition'. In *Middle English Alliterative Poetry and its Literary Background: Seven Essays*. Ed. David Lawton. Cambridge, 70–87, 140–42.

Bawcutt, Priscilla J. 1998. 'Crossing the Border: Scottish Poetry and English Readers in the Sixteenth Century'. In Mapstone and Wood, 59–76.

Beattie, W. 1974. 'Some Early Scottish Books'. In *The Scottish Tradition: Essays in Honour of Roland Gordon Cant.* Ed. G. W. S. Barrow. Edinburgh, 107–20.

Bradbury, Nancy H. 2011. 'Representations of Peasant Speech: Some Literary and Social Contexts for *The Taill of Rauf Coilȝear*'. In *Medieval Romance, Medieval Contexts*. Ed. Rhiannon Purdie and Michael Cichon. Cambridge, 19–33.

Caughey, Anna 2013. '"Methink it.grete skill": Conciliatory Chivalry in Three Fifteenth-Century Scottish Romances'. In *Fresche Fontanis: Studies in the Culture of Medieval and Early Modern Scotland.* Ed. Janet H. Williams and J. Derrick McClure. Newcastle upon Tyne, 97–111.

Clay, Rotha M. 1909. *The Medieval Hospitals of England.* London.

Cowan, Ian B. and David E. Easson 1976. *Medieval Religious Houses, Scotland: with an appendix on the houses in the Isle of Man.* 2nd edn. London.

Craigie, William A. 1942. 'The Scottish Alliterative Poems'. *Proceedings of the British Academy* 28, 217–36.

Cross, Roseanna 2009. *Time Past Well Remembered; The Handling of Time in Some Middle English and Old French Texts*. Saarbrücken.

Crossley, Pamela K. 1999. Review article. *Speculum* 74, 445–47.

Dickson, Robert and John P. Edmond 1890. *Annals of Scottish Printing from the introduction of the art in 1507 to the beginning of the seventeenth century.* Cambridge.

Duff, E. Gordon 1893, rev. Lotte Hellinga 2009. *Printing in England in the Fifteenth Century: E. Gordon Duff's bibliography, with supplementary descriptions, chronologies and a census of copies*. London.

Fein, Susanna G. 1992. 'Form and Continuity in the Alliterative Tradition: Cruciform Design and Double Birth in Two Stanzaic Poems'. *Modern Language Quarterly* 53, 100–25.

Fradenburg, Louise O. 1991. *City, Marriage, Tournament: Arts of Rule in Late Medieval Scotland*. Madison, WI.

Gray, Douglas 2008. *Later Medieval English Literature*. Oxford.

Hardman, Phillipa and Marianne Ailes 2017. *The Legend of Charlemagne in Medieval England: The Matter of France in Middle English and Anglo-Norman Literature.* Cambridge.

Harris, Joel 1977. 'The King in Disguise: An International Popular Tale in Two Old Icelandic Adaptations'. *Arkiv för Nordisk Filologi* 94, 57–81.

Jacobs, Nicolas 1972. 'Alliterative Storms: A Topos in Middle English'. *Speculum* 47, 675–719.

Kindrick, Robert 1984. 'Politics and Poetry at the Court of James III'. *Studies in Scottish Literature* 19, 40–55.

Klein, Andrew W. 2017. 'Scots Take the Wheel: The Problem of Period and the Medieval Scots Alliterative Thirteen-Line Stanza'. *Studies in Scottish Literature* 43, 15–21.

Lindsay, Sarah 2015. 'The Courteous Monster: Chivalry, Violence, and Social Control in *The Carl of Carlisle*'. *Journal of English and Germanic Philology* 114, 401–18.

Lucas, Peter J. 1997. '"A Testimonye of Verye Ancient Tyme"? Some Models for the Parkerian Anglo-Saxon Type Designs'. In *Of the Making of Books: medieval manuscripts, their scribes and readers: essays presented to M. B. Parkes*. Ed. P. R. Robinson and Rivkah Zim. Aldershot, 147–88.

MacDonald, Alasdair A. 1998. 'Early Modern Scottish Literature and the Parameters of Culture'. In Mapstone and Wood, 77–100.

Mainer, Sergi 2010. *The Scottish Romance Tradition, c. 1375–c. 1550: Nation, Chivalry, and Knighthood.* New York and Amsterdam, 249–55.

Mann, Alastair J. 2000. *The Scottish Book Trade 1500–1720.* East Linton.

Mapstone, Sally 1986. 'The Advice to Princes Tradition in Scottish Literature, 1450–1500'. Unpub. D.Phil. thesis, Oxford.

—— and Juliette Wood, eds. 1998. *The Rose and the Thistle: Essays on the Culture of Late Medieval and Renaissance Scotland.* East Linton.

McDiarmid, Matthew P. 1991. '*Rauf Colyear*, *Golagros and Gawane*, Hary's *Wallace*: Their Themes of Independence and Religion'. *Studies in Scottish Literature* 26, 328–33.

Morris, Margaret K. 1992. 'Generic Oxymoron in *The Tale of Rauf Coilȝear*'. In *Voices in Translation: The Authority of 'Olde Bookes' in Medieval Literature: Essays in Honor of Helaine Newstead.* Ed. Deborah Sinnreich-Levi and Gale Sigal. New York, 137–55.

Neilson, George 1903. *Huchown of the Awle Ryale, the Alliterative Poet: A Historical Criticism of Fourteenth Century Poems Ascribed to Sir Hew of Eglintoun.* Glasgow.

Papworth, John W. 1961. *Papworth's Ordinary of British Armorials.* London.

Pollock, Sean 2009. 'Border States: Parody, Sovereignty, and Hybrid Identity in *The Carl of Carlisle*'. *Arthuriana* 19.2, 10–26.

Purdie, Rhiannon 2006. 'Medieval Romance in Scotland'. In *A Companion to Medieval Scottish Poetry*. Ed. Priscilla Bawcutt and Janet H. Williams. Cambridge, 165–77.

Putter, Ad 2012. 'Ralph the Collier'. In *Heroes and Anti-Heroes in Medieval Romance*. Ed. Neil Cartlidge. Cambridge, 145–58.

Ramsay, Lee C. 1983. *Chivalric Romances: Popular Literature in Medieval England.* Bloomington, IN.

Riddy, Felicity 1988. 'The Alliterative Revival'. In *The History of Scottish Literature, Volume I: Origins to 1660 (Medieval and Renaissance)*. Ed. R. D. S. Jack. Aberdeen, 39–54 (see also Bawcutt 1987).

Royan, Nicola 2010. 'The Alliterative *Awntyrs* Stanza in Older Scots Verse'. In *Medieval Alliterative Poetry: Essays in Honour of Thorlac Turville-Petre*. Ed. John A. Burrow and Hoyt N. Duggan. Dublin, 185–94.

Schiff, Randy 2012. 'Sovereign Exception: Pre-National Consolidation in *The Taill of Rauf Coilyear*'. In *The Anglo-Scottish Border and the Shaping of Identity, 1300–1600*. Ed. Mark P. Bruce and Katherine H. Terrell. New York, 33–50.

Shepherd, Geoffrey 1970. 'The Nature of Alliterative Poetry in Late Medieval England', *Proceedings of the British Academy* 56, 57–76.

Shepherd, S[tephen] H. A. 1991, '"Of thy glitterand gyde haue I na gle": *The Taill of Rauf Coilyear*'. *Archiv für das Studium der neueren Sprachen und Literaturen* 228, 284–98.

Smith, John T. 1807. *Antiquities of Westminster.* London.

Smyser, H. M. 1932. '*The Taill of Rauf Coilyear* and its Sources'. *Harvard Studies and Notes in Philology and Literature* 14, 135–50.

—— 1967. 'Charlemagne Legends'. In *A Manual of the Writings in Middle English, 1050–1500, Volume 1 Romances*. Gen. ed. J. Burke Severs. New Haven, CT, 80–100, 256–66.

Snell, Rachel 2000. 'The Undercover King'. In *Medieval Insular Romance: Translation and Innovation*. Ed. Judith Weiss *et al*. Cambridge, 133–54.

Stuhmiller, Jacqueline 2013. 'Poaching and Carnival'. *The Book of Nature and Humanity in the Middle Ages and the Renaissance*. Ed. David Hawkes *et al*. Turnhout, 183–207.

Tristram, E. W., ed. Eileen Tristram 1955. *English Wall Painting in the Fourteenth Century*. London.

Turville-Petre, Thorlac 1974. '"Summer Sunday", "De tribus regibus mortuis", and "the Awntyrs off Arthure": Three Poems in the Thirteen-Line Stanza'. *Review of English Studies* 25, 1–14.

—— 1977. *The Alliterative Revival*. Cambridge: D. S. Brewer.

Vincent, Diane 2010. 'Reading a Christian–Saracen Debate in Fifteenth-Century Middle English Charlemagne Romance: The Case of *Turpines Story*'. In *The Exploitations of Medieval Romance*. Ed. Laura Ashe *et al*. Cambridge, 90–107.

Walsh, Elizabeth 1975. 'The King in Disguise'. *Folklore* 86, 3–24.

—— 1979. '*The Taill of Rauf Coilyear*: Oral Motif in Literary Guise'. *Scottish Literary Journal* 6.2, 5–19.

—— 1991. 'Upward Bound: The Sociopolitical Significance of the King in Disguise Motif'. *Studies in Scottish Literature* 26, 157–63.

Watry, Paul B. 1993. 'Sixteenth Century Printing Types and Ornaments of Scotland with an Introductory Survey of the Scottish Book Trade'. Unpub. D.Phil. Diss., Oxford [BodL MS D.Phil. c.10583].

Whiting, B. J. 1949–51. 'Proverbs and Proverbial Sayings from Scottish Writings Before 1600'. *Mediaeval Studies* 11, 123–205; 13, 87–164.

Wright, Glenn 2001. 'Churl's Courtesy: *Rauf Coilȝear* and its English Analogues'. *Neophilologus* 85, 647–62.

—— 2002. 'Convention and Conversion: The Saracen Ending of *The Taill of Rauf Coilzear*'. *Al-Masaq* 14, 100–12.

Glossary

In most substantive respects, this glossary can function as a concordance. I have, however, limited myself to five instances of the banal/commonplace, usually 'function words'. Although I have built in extensive cross-references, readers may find it easier to cross-check common OSc variant forms, for example *a/ai*. In the alphabetical arrangement, *y* to represent a vowel is intercalated with *i*, as is *þ* (thorn) with *th*; *i* representing consonantal *j* follows *i*; *u/v/w* have been alphabetised according to value, whether vowel *u*, consonant *v* or semi-vowel *w*; *ȝ* (yogh) follows semi-vowel *y*. Given the intensely colloquial character of much of the poem, I frequently use the abbreviation '*lit.*' to introduce a literal rendition of the form, before providing a translation more idiomatic in modern English.

All readings discussed in the notes are marked 'n', and emended readings are starred.

Grammatical Abbreviations

adj.	adjective	phrs.	phrase
adv.	adverb	pl.	plural
art.	article	poss.	possessive
aux.	auxiliary	pp.	past participle
comp.	comparative	pres.p.	present participle
conj.	conjunction	prep.	preposition
demon.	demonstrative	pres.	present
impers.	impersonal	pron.	pronoun
indef.	indefinite	refl.	reflexive
interj.	interjection	sg.	singular
n.	noun	subj.	subjunctive
num.	numeral	super.	superlative
obj.	object(ive case)	v.	verb, the infinitive

abaisit *v.pp.* abashed, dismayed 101
abyde *v.* to wait for, to endure or stand up to, to take up a stand 282, 485, 805
about *adv*. all round (the table), scattered around 215, 669, 682
about *prep.* around 34, 471
abufe *adv.* at the top 43, 678, 858; *prep.* above 815
afraid *adj*. afraid, frightened 878
affray *n.* occasion for fear or alarm 507
agane *adv.* again, anew, in return 155, 158, 204, 422, 622, 626, 861; *prep.* in anticipation of 322; **agayne** *prep*. toward 607
aganis *prep.* against, in opposition to 32
ay *adv.* always, continually 692, 908, 940
air *adv.* previously 158, 823; **airar** *comp.* earlier, sooner 545
air *n.* heir 931
airly *adj*. early 322, 777; **airlie** *adv.* 272, 363
airt *n.* compass-point 137, 329
all *adj*. all, every, entire 7, 9, 48, 52, 105, 218, 231, 274, 328, 341 etc.; *as n.* everything, every way 268, 384, 435, 621, 639; as *n.pl.* 167, 578, 893, 970; *phrs.* ~ **thay** all those 7
all *adv.* completely, continuously 28, 35, 101, 196, 268, 661, 693, 735; *phrs.* **at ~ richt** thoroughly properly 685
allace *interj*. alas 708
allane *adj*. alone 370, 611
almaist *adv.* almost 831; *phrs.* **not (= nocht)...** ~ almost nothing, insignificant 651
als *adv*. also 303, 523, 757, 931
als *conj.* just as (usually in the coordinated construction **als...as**) 108, 252, 262, 332, 910; *cf.* **as**
alswa *adv.* similarly 115
am *see* **be**
amang *prep.* among, amidst 22, 37, 69, 419, 623, 657, 781, 788
amend *v.* to amend, better things 253
anamalit *v.pp*. painted (in enamel) 684
and *conj.* most usually 'and', but instances meaning '(even) if' 56, 146, 241, 294, 312, 370, 440, 511, 603, 876, 913, 928
ane *num.art.* a(n), (the numeral) one, single 2, 3, 15, 25, 42, 43, etc.; **a** 863; *as n.* a single one or person 114, 611, 625; a certain person 620; *as adj.* alone 260; *phrs*. **of** ~ most [adj.] of any single person, of that sort 236, 575; **the tane** = **that ane** 885
anent *prep.adv*. opposite 278
anerly *adv.* solely, merely 589, 844
aneuch *adv.* enough, aplenty, a sufficiency 160, 187, 201, 249, 525, 687; **anew** *adj.* (an) appropriate or sufficient (amount to fill the baskets) 365
ane-vther *pron.adj.* another 504, 841; cf. **vther mony ane** many another/others 3

anew *see* **aneuch**
anger *n.* rage 156; **angeris** *pl.* anxious or testing situations 944
angerit *v.pp.* enraged 830
anhertance *n.* adherents, followers *534n
anis *adv.* once, one time 126, 643, 691n, 693; **at** ~ mixed together 473
anournit *v.pp.* adorned, ornamented 688
answer *n.* answer, response 54, 224
appeirit *v.pt.* came into view 350; **appeirand** *pp.adj.* apparent, proximate 931;
apperrellit *v. pp.* adorned *663n
ar *see* **be**
arguit *v.pt.* debated, argued 643
arme-banis *n.pl.* arms 470
armour *n.* armour 770; **armouris** *pl.* pieces of plate 772
array *n.* clothing, equipment 478, 480, 549, 778, 791, 934
arrayis *v.pres. 3sg.* (*refl.*) **thame** ~, clothes or adorns themselves 351; **him arrayit** *pt.* 575
art *see* **be**
as *conj.* as, while 14, 46, 67, 70, 132, 172, 176, 187, 252, 261, etc.; as if 731; *cf.* **als**
asking *n.* question(s), interrogation 224
askis *v.pres.1, 3sg.* ask 617, 941
assay *n.* trial, attack 392
assay *v.* to try 302
assaill *v.* to attack 825
assent *n.* consent, assent 392
assigne *v.* to assign, designate to 756
at *conj.* that 268
ather *pron.adj.* each, either 289, 825, 832
atour *prep.* above 391; **attour** *adv.* 467
aucht *v.pres.subj.* should, ought 126
auld *adj.* old 517, 559
away *adv.* absent, away, to a distance 274, 526, 603, 814, 824
awin *adj.* own 33, 68, 113, 377, 635; *n.* possessions, things 128

bacheleiris *n.pl.* youthful knights, knights in training 11
bad, *see* **bid**
baid *n.* waiting, delay 486
baid, *see* **byde**
bayne *adv.* readily, eagerly 605
bair *adj.* empty, desolate 797, 901
bair *n.* boar 185
bair *see* **beir**

bait *v.pt.* (*lit.* bit, but perhaps beat) struck (and dented) 821n
baith *num.adv.pron.* both (two), also, including 10, 48, 58, 84, 92, 96, 104, 250, 267, 280, etc.
bak *n.* 'back-up', aid, support 844; **on** ~ *adv.* back, backwards, away 695
bakin *v.pp.* baked 209
bald *adj. as n.* bold one 407, 711
bald *adv.* vigorously 222
baldly *adv.* boldly, fearlessly 805, 882
bancouris *n.pl.* tapestries for covering furniture 682
band *v.pt.* bound, tied 796
band *n.* contract *562n; **bandis** *pl.* door-hinges or -hasps 628
bane *adj.* obedient 420
barrounis *n.pl.* barons, lords 11
basnet *n.* helmet 462; **basnetis** *pl.* 821
battall *n.* battle 827
batteris *v.imper.pl.* strike 882
be *prep.* by (in its various senses) 8, 97, 118, 123, 144, 180, 235, 252, 257, 259, etc.; to the extent of 34; *conj.* by the time that 23, 29, 383; ~ **that** 38
be *v.* to be, exist, occur, frequently as 'have'-auxiliary with verbs of motion 56 (2nd use), 70, 71, 124, 163, 209, 288, 293, 297, 308, etc.; **am** *pres.1sg.* 106, 129n, 173, 247 (2x), etc.; **art** *pres.2sg.* 94, 122, 127, 159, 233 (2x), etc.; **is** *pres.3sg.* 87, 89, 134, 166, 167, etc.; *pres.pl.* 58; **ar** *pres.pl.* 74, 103, 179, 523, 559, etc.; **be** *imper.* 546; *pres.subj.* 56, 164, 256, 282, 398, etc.; **war** *pres.subj.* should or would (have to) be 57, 109, 147, 285, 379, etc.; **was** *v. pt.sg.* was 23, 31, 33, 34, 40, etc.; *pt.pl.* were 6, 131, ?143, 712; **was** as both sg. and pl. (and as mark of pluperfect, as again 349) 29; **war** *pt.pl.* 20, 91, 181, 184, 274, etc.; **bene** *pp.* 119, 170 (2x), 205, 230, etc.; *phrs.* **be al that** whatever 435
becum *v.imper.* become 889
bed *n.* bed 261, 264, 269
befoir *adv.* ahead, in front of, previously 121, 461; *prep.* 4, 119, 199, 240, 355, 400, 751, 847
beget *v.* to deceive 604n
begylit *v.pp.* deceived 709
begin *v.* to begin, start or head, emerge or shoot forth 98, 145, 213, 626, 769; *pres.pl.* (for *future*) 130; **began** *pt.* 140, 225, 456; *pp.* 360; **begouth** *pt.* began, prepared 120
behaldand *v.pres.p.* looking at, watching 416; **beheld** *pt.* 454
behind *adv.* behind 65
behouit *v.pt.* it was necessary (for him) 405; *cf.* **byrd**
behufe *n.* use 41; **behuse** *pl.* 82
beir *v.* to bear (in various senses, incl. sustain, hold, perform, display an armorial device) 287; **beiris** *v.pres.pl.* 562; **bair** *pt.* 223, 455, 516; **borne** *pp.* born 561

beird *v.pt.* lit. roared, spoke 175
beirne *n.* warrior 729, 780, 857; **beirnis** *pl.* 187, 561, 821
beliue *adv.* promptly, immediately 94, 112, 263, 324, 612, 628
bellis *n.pl.* bells 532
bellisand *adj.* embellished, beautiful 476
ben *adv.* within, inwards 696
bene *adj.* fine, wonderful 678
bene *pp. see* **be**
bennysoun *n.* blessing; *phrs.* **for my** ~ to drink to my health 212
bent *n.* (*lit.* grass) plain, open space 729, 796, 811
benwart *adv.* inwards, inside 131
beriall *n.* beryl 463; **beriallis** *pl.* 472
beseik *v.pres.1sg.* beseech, ask, pray 768, 941
besyde *adv.* in addition 784
besyde *prep.* beside, next to 702
best *adj.super.* best 359, 928; *as n.* the best sort/thing 111, 134, 209, 779; *phrs.* **the** ~ with your best skill, as skilfully as you can (a fossilised instrumental?) 882
bestiall *n.* animals 678
bet *v.pp.* mended, replenished 142
betaucht *v.pt.* committed (it to) 771
betakin *v.* to mean, indicate 403
betyde *v.pt.* (impersonal) there befell (him) 15
betyme *adv.* promptly, seasonably 287
better *adj.comp.* better 31, 62, 243, 430; *adv.comp.* 110, 258
betwene *adv.* intermittently, here and there 664; *prep.* 869
by *adv.* near, beside 561, 857
bid *v.pres.1sg.* command 165, 313; *imper.* 625; **bad** *pt.* 113, 132, 175, 423, 486, 596, 740
bidding *n.* (my) command 124, 176, 420, 435, 584
byde *v.* to stay, remain (exposed), wait, endure 285, 780, 963; **baid** *pt.* 28, 797
bigging *n.* building, house 188; **biggingis** *pl.* 901
byrd *v.pres.2sg.* ought (to) 160; *cf.* **behouit**
byrdis *n.pl.*[1] birds 209, 678
byrdis *n.pl.*[2] ladies 532
byre *n.* barn 111
byrnand *v.pres.p.* burning, shining 188; *cf.* **bricht-byrnand**
birny *n.* shirt of mail 763, 805
bischop *n.* bishop 343; **bischoppis** *pl.* 339, 954
blak *adj.* discoloured (from lack of use) 522
blame *n.* blame, rebuke 101, 162, 237
blan *see* **blin**
blandit *v.pp.* (*lit.* mixed) scattered over 472
blaw *n.* blow 369

blenkit *v.pt.* glanced, looked aside 850
blew *v.pt.* blew 16; blew or drove apart 28n; *phrs.* **greit boist** ~ spoke with great arrogance 369
blin *v.* to leave off or stop 92, 628; **blan** *v.pt.* 821
blyth *adj.* happy, pleased 75, 678, 850; **blyith** 192, 216, 407
blonk *n.* horse, mount 796, 806 (a camel); **blonkis** *pl.* 562
blude *n.* blood 857
bocht *v.pt.* purchased, redeemed 717; *phrs.* **be him þat me** ~ in Jesus's (the redeemer's) name 180; *phrs.* ~ **it deir** paid a heavy price for it 370
body *n.* body 550
bodword *n.* message 901
boist *n.* an arrogant speech 369, 881
boistit *v.pt.* threateningly commanded 780
bone *adj.* good 551
bordourit *v.pp.* bound about (ornamentally) 462
borne *see* **beir**
bot *adv.* only 57, 112, 260, 441, 505, 552, 634, 781, 891, 895, etc.; *conj.* the adversative 'yet' 83, 271, 311, 436, 508, 561, etc.; except, unless, without 367, 447, 558, 612; **bot gif** 497, 537n, 539, 548, 936 (but, if); **bot, but** *prep.* except, without 31, 68, 184, 413, 499, 517, 663, 844
boun *adj.* ready, prepared 124, 881; *adv.* readily, directly 792
boun *v.* to take one's course, hasten 396, 423
bowre *n.* private apartments 532
braid *adj.* large, broad 805; *phrs.* **on breid** abroad, out of doors 593
braid *n.* breadth, distance 34n; **breid** 152
braid *n.* stroke 857
braidit *v.pt.* jerked, drew 863
braissaris *n.pl.* armour for the arm 471
braissit *v.pp.* (*lit.* embraced), clasped 550
braithlie *adv.* violently, strongly 175
brand *n.* sword 518, 763, 805, 857; **brandis** *pl.* 522
brand *n.* piece of wood 909; **brandis** *pl.* 131
braun *n.* flesh 185
breid *n.* bread 185, 209
breid *see* **braid**
breif *v.imper.* speak (to), address 881n
brest *v.pt.* burst, flowed 858
bricht *adj.* bright, colourful, shining, glowing 131, 471, 550, 682, 909; *adv.* brightly 188, 462
bricht-byrnand *adj.* bright-burning 132, 222
brydill *n.* bridle 476
bring *v.* to bring (in its various senses, e.g., conduct) 59, 83, 305, 420, 646, 844, 954; *imper.* 64, 300, 399, 561; **brocht** *pt.* 185, 269, 276; *pp.* 452, 489, 596, 901, 909

brokin *v.pp.* broken, violated 843
broun *adj.* brown (bare of grass at Christmas) 796
browdin *v.pp.* embroidered 682
browis *n.pl.* eyebrows 858
buik *n.* book, source 353; **buikis** *pl.* in *phrs.* **be ~ and bellis** I tell you seriously (*lit.* a reference to the anathema of excommunication) 532
buird *n.* board, table 145, 158, 185; **buirdis** *pl.* 725
buklair *n.* round shield 517
burelie *adj.* strong, excellent 188; **burely** 264
burgh *n.* walled town, fortress 396
burneist *v.pp.* burnished 462n
busk *n.* bush 796
buskit *v.pt.refl.* prepared for departure, hastened 273, 407, 593
busteous *adj.* rough, crude, discourteous 729, 780
busteously *adv.* roughly, rudely 593
but *adv.* outside 111
but *see* **bot**
bute *n.* remedy *31n

cachit *see* **catche**
cair *n.* care, sorrow 912
cairful *adj.* filled with care, anxious 714
cais *n.* chance; *phrs.* **in** ~ on the chance (that) 254, 260
call *v.* to call 582; **cal** 238; **call** *pres.1sg.* 754; *pres.pl.* 836; *imper.* 291, 436, 889; *pres.subj.* 637; **callis** *pres.pl.* 46; **callit** *pt.* 133, 157, 278, 359, 390, 583, 956
cameill *n.* camel 803
can *v.pres.* to know (how) 621; can 644; *subj.* 61
can *v.aux.* 'did' 700, 825
cant *adj.* lively, brisk 42, 113
cantlie *adv.* briskly, speedily 386; **cantly** 803
capill *n.* nag 43, 114, 365, 382, 418, 487, 613, 637
capouns *n.pl.* capons 111; **capounis** 207
caryit *v.pt.* journeyed, went 951
carll *n.* peasant, rustic 42, 44, 93, 100, 132, 148, 194, 211, 278, 280, 446, 454, 603, 745, 787
carping *n.* conversation 727
carpis *v.pres.2sg.* speak 492; **carpit** *pt.* 44, 194, 211
carpitit *v.pp.* covered with rugs *680n
cast *n.* design, stratagem 33
cast *v.imper.* throw off 487; **cassin** *pp.* unloaded 613; *see* **kest**
catche *v.* to proceed, go, pass 496; **cachit** *pt.* proceeded, went 33; **catchit** 382; **caucht** 837; **chachand** *pres.p.* 42; **(on) catchand** 386
catche *v.* to seize, attach 526; **caucht** *pt.* 382

chace *v.* to drive 902
chachand *see* **catche**
chaip *v.* to escape, go away 558; *pres.1sg.* 720
chaip *v.pres.1sg.* to sell 719
chalmer *n.* chamber, private quarters 235, 263, 770
chance *n.* set of circumstances or events 720
changes *v.pres.3sg.* changes, transforms 720
charcoill *n.* (store of) charcoal 320
chauffray *n.* 'chaffer', wares, goods for trade 321
cheif *adj.* chief, primary 295; ~ **tyme** *phrs.* (period of) ascendancy 1
cheir *n.* countenance, manner, bearing 192, 216, 348, 407, 720, 839; *phrs.* **maid...gude** ~ encouraged rejoicing 178 (cf. 348)
cheualry *n.* chivalry, good breeding 295; **cheualrie** a band of knights 341
cheualrous *adj.* chivalrous 839
cheueris *v.pres.pl.* shake, shiver 96
chiftane *n.* leader, commander 1
chyld *n.* servant, attendant 235
chin *n.* the chin 96
chosin *pp.adj.* excellent, noble 1
circulit *v.pp.* encircled, bordered 475, 676
clais *n.pl.* cloth(e)s 432, 705
clamis *v.pres.3sg.* has legal claim to 926
cled *v.pp.* clothed, equipped with covering 265, 680, 704
cleikit *v.pt.* snatched, pulled 819
cleir *adj.* clear, fair, distinct, beautiful 211, 290, 472, 495, 715, 957; *adv.* plainly, distinctly, brightly 194, 470; *as n.* resplendent man 705
clene *adj.* purified, bright 705
clene *adv.* cleanly, completely 125, 680
clething *n.* clothing 704
clois *adj.* close-fitting, enclosing 772
closit *v.pp.* enclosed 265; **closand** *pres.p.* 681
coft *v.pp.* bought, purchased 105
coilȝear *n.* charcoal man 55, 118, 121, 126, 145, 175, 183, 204, 217, 220, 227, 238, 267, 293, 307, 316, 319, 364, 417, 421, 428, 486, 488, 516, 538, 546, 555, 557, 571, 633, 638, 651, 714, 731; **coilȝearis** *poss.* 92, 601; *see also* **Rauf Coilȝear** *in Index of Proper Names*
coilis *n.pl.* coals, charcoal 50, 305; **coillis** 365, 594
columbyn *n*, columbine 671
come *see* **cum**
command *v.pp.* commanded (to do) 501, 584
commandment *n.* commandment, order(s) 390, 453; **commandement** 438
commounis *n.pl.* common people 340, 429

company *n.* companionship, group of companions, troop; **cumpany** 294, 775; *phrs.* **company bair** performed (proper) duties of fellowship, comported himself (properly) 223
compeir *v.* to appear in a law court 198, 497
conditioun *n.* the agreed compact, conditions set for an engagement 843
confound *v.* to overcome, overthrow 871
conseruit *v.pt.* maintained 949
conuent *n.(pl.)* convents (perhaps 'dozens'?) 344
conuert *v.* to convert 920; *pres.subj.* 890
cornellis *n.pl.* corners 681
counsall *n.* counsel, advice 299, 367, 583, 746, 962
counsall *v.pres.1sg.* advise, counsel 526
counsingis *n.pl.* 'cousins', relations or companions, like-minded individuals 896; **cussingis** 912
countenance *n.* bearing, manner, appearance 714, 804; *phrs.* **held gude countenance** preserved a proper bearing 223
counteris *v.pres.pl.* encounter, wage battle 871
countit *v.pt.* accounted, reckoned, appraised 651
countrie *n.* neighbourhood 325, 410, 446
cours *n.* running, turn in a joust 812
coursour *n.* steed, noble mount 114
court *n.* court (the institution, its members, and the place it gathers) 30, 33, 232, 241, 246, 260, 290, 299, 305, 314, 371, 388, 496, 534, 638, 951
courtasie *n.* courtesy, proper behaviour 125, 171, 423, 429, 718, 745
courteir *n.* courtier 163
courtes *adj.* courteous 163, 715
courtesly *adv.* courteously, in a humble fashion 421
courtingis *n.pl.* curtains (a tester) 265
couth *v.pt.* knew 171; *pt.subj.* 125
couer *v.* to heal, recover 921
couerit *v.pp.* covered 680
crabitnes *n.* rancour, ill humour 526
craft *n.* profession 301
craue *v.* to plead, ask for; *phrs.* **that sall not be to** ~ there's no pleading about it, it is not open to discussion 496
creillis *n.pl.* baskets 43, 365, 382, 418, 487, 613
creip *v.* *lit.* to crawl, to be subservient, or behave in a subservient manner 126
cry *v.* to call (upon) 945
cristallis *n.pl.* crystals 472
Cristin *adj.* Christian 171, 746, 871, 889, 943; as *n.pl.* 912
cristinnit *v.pp.* baptised 495
cruell *adj.* fierce, stern, violent 804
cule *v.* to cool, refresh (himself) 836

cum *v.* to come, extend 241, 247, 317, 501, 511, 571, 614, 722; *pres.1sg.* 638; *pres.subj.* 254, 260; *imper.* 299, 583; **cummis** *pres.3sg.* 759; *pres. pl.* 430; **cummand** *pres.p.* 343, 607, 681, 800, 840; **cumming** 397; **come** *pt.* 42, 120, 326, 340, 417, 570, 572, 657, 718, 803, etc.; **cummin** *pp.* 107, 785
cumlie *adj.* handsome 199, 470; **cumly** 715; *adv.* in a fitting manner 194, 265n; as *n.pl.* 573
cumming *n.* arrival 580, 952
cumpany *see* **company**
cunnand *n.* covenant, pledge 319, 387, 537; **cunnandis** *pl.* 544
cunnand *v.pres.p.adj.* knowing, canny, trained 163
cunning *n.* knowledge; *phrs.* **had** ~ knew 93
cunningis *n,pl.* rabbits 207
cup *n.* goblet 212
cuplit *v.pp.* joined 43
curagious *adj.* courageous, brave 740, 766, 804
cussanis *n.pl.* armour covering the thigh 470
cussingis *see* **counsingis**

day *n.* day, dawn 23, 95, 135, 272, 324, 342, 363, 383, 404, 490, 494, 513, 545, 587, 694, 795, 798, 828, 847, 923, 954; **dayes** *poss.* 105; **dayis** *pl.* 357 (accusative of extent of time); **the** ~ (dative of time) today 401, 604, 645
daillis *n.pl.* valleys 383, 414, 794
daynteis *n.pl.* good or rich things (to eat), delicacies or delicately worked things 189; **danteis** 675
dayntelie *see* **dantely**
dame *n.* lady, wife 94, 102, 105, 107, 376, 716
dantely *adv.* carefully, elegantly 664, 675; **dayntelie** 189
dantit *v.pt.* conquered, intimidated 597; *pp.* 433
dar *v.pres.1sg.* dare 374; **durst** *pt.* 99, 485, 597
dawis *v.pres.3sg.* dawns, grows light 922; **dew** *pt.* 363n; **dawin** *pp.* 383
debait *n.* strife, conflict; *phrs.* **withoutin** ~ there's no denying it (but perhaps peacefully, politely) 44n
defend *v.pres.1sg.* prohibit, forbid 60, 524
degre *n.* rank, status 767
deid *adj.* dead 512, 813, 817, 961
deid *n.* deed(s), action 271, 694; **deidis** *pl.* 513
deill *v.* to exchange (blows), deal (with) 512, 597
deip *adj.* deep 17
deir *adj.* dear or honoured, expensive 463, 513, 752
deir *adv.* expensively, with difficulty 105, 252, 370, 717
deir *n.* deer 196
deis *n.* dais; *phrs.* **on deis** for the table 189

delay n. delay 531, 539; *phrs.* **mak na** ~ come quickly 300
deliuer *v.imper.* ~ **the** exert yourself, act quickly 300
dell *n.* valley 17
deme *v.* to judge, scrutinise 674
dentit *v.pp.* indented, inlaid 664
derf *adj.* harsh, difficult (to cross) 383
derffly *adv.* vigorously 794
desyre *n.* wish 109
deuill *n.* devil 718; *phrs.* **quhy** ~ why in the hell? 95
deuise *v.pres.1sg.* tell 611
dew *see* **dawis**
dyamountis *n.pl.* diamonds 464, 664
dicht *v.* to prepare, display, spread out 133; *pp.* 142, 189, 587, 674, 675, 684, 795
die *v.* to die 950
digne *adj.* worthy, appropriate, stately 352, 752, 954
ding *v.* to strike 914
dyntes *n.pl.* blows 512
discouerand *v.pres.p.* reconnoitring (to find if) 794
dispair *n.* despair, doubt 929n
dispittously *adv.* without pity, mercilessly 900
disseuer *v.* to separate 525; **disseuerit** *pp.* 29
distroy *v.* destroy 748
diuers *adj.* diverse, various 675
do *v.* to act (in accord with), perform, place or put, cause, complete 368, 543, 789, 820; *imper.* 112, 165, 299, 436; *pres.1sg.* 259, 929; **dois** *pres.2sg.* 86, 895; *imper.* 193; **done** *pp.* 176, 283, 352, 513, 572, 584, 843, 867; *phrs.* **to** ~ **ȝow in his gentrise** to put yourself at (the mercy ascribed to) his good breeding 368; ~ **way** leave off, shut up 434
docht *v.pt.* availed, was good; *phrs.* ~ **nocht to do** was good for nothing 789
dosouris *n.pl.* hangings, arras 674
douchereis *n.pl.* dukedoms, duchies 922, 932
douchtie *adj.* doughty, courageous; as *n.* doughty, warlike man 587, 694, 795, 954
doun *adv.* down 111, 177, 197, 333, 914; *phrs.* **gang** ~ to set (of the sun) 923
doun *n.* hill(s) 414, 794
dourly *adv.* resolutely, with severity 914
dout *n.* fear 824, 965
draif *v.pt.* poured down 17; *phrs.* ~ **on** rushed, moved speedily 27
dreichlie *adv.* steadily, deeply 215
dreid *n.* fear 79; anticipating harm (to) 196, 376
dreid *v.pres.1sg.* *(and refl.)* am afraid 237, 597, 709
drest *v.pp.* placed, prepared 199, 406
drew *v.pt.* passed, approached 38

drift *n.* driving snow *17n
drink *n.* beverage 81
drink *v.* to drink 261; *imper.* 213; **drank** *pt.* 215
dubbit *v.pt.* dubbed, invested (with knighthood) 751
duchepeiris *n.pl. lit.* Charlemagne's *douze pers* (his twelve great lords), great nobles 10
duches *n.* duchess 926, 957
dukis *n.pl.* dukes, military leaders 10, 752
dule *n.* lament, distress 95, 199
durandlie *adv.* lastingly, continuously 17
during *v.pres.p.* enduring, lasting 923
dure *n.* door 94, 102, 120; **duris** *pl.* 674
durst *see* **dar**
dwell *v.* to stay or remain, tarry, have one's home 21, 49, 232; **dwel** *pres.1sg.* 915; **dwellis** *pres.2sg.* 234; *pres.3sg.* 534
dwelling *n.* delay, tardiness (at getting home) 237

e *n.* eye 692, 714
efter *adv.* after(wards), later 251, 511, 536
efter *prep.* after 135, 221, 346, 582, 617, 620, 692, 836, 966
eik *adv.* also 208
eir *n.* ear 150
eird *n.* the earth, the floor, land 153, 171
eirnestly *adv.* with seriousness 617, 692
eis *n.* ease; *phrs.* **maid thame** ~ gotten themselves comfortable 220
eismentis *n.pl.* comforts 82
eist *n.* east 16, 27, 137
ellis *adv.* otherwise 127, 538
empreouris *n.pl.* commanders, nobles (not an exact royal title) 3
enchaip *v.* to practise trading 316
encheif *v.* to achieve, triumph 316
end *n.* end, death 919, 949
endlang *prep.* all along, the length of 686
engreif *v.* to (a)grieve, create anger or be angered 616; **engreuit** *pp.* 600
enteris *v.pres.pl.* enter 189
erand *n.* errand, assigned task 535, 545
erlis *n.pl.* noblemen 3
euer *adv.* ever, always 224, 361, 362, 482, 707, 802, 914, 950
euermair *adv.* forever 938, 968
euill *adj.* evil, bad, unpleasant 95, 135, 168, 746; *adv.* badly, not at all 40, 834, 917
euin *adv.* directly 792
excuse *v.* defend or exempt (from blame) 84

face *n.pl.* foes, enemies 850; **fais** 750

fay *n.* faith 888; *phrs.* **in/be my (gude)** ~ surely, truly 88, 97, 509, 568; **of thy bone** ~ of your sincerity, of your fidelity to your word 551n

failʒe *v.pres.pl.* become exhausted, lose all strength 831

faindis *v.pres.2sg.* are attempting or trying 898

faine *v.pt.* stopped, ceased *153n

faynt *adj.* weak 523

fair *adj.* pleasant, clear, noble, beautiful 8, 289, 523, 775, 930, 967

fair *n.* fare, provision 112, 206; behaviour, gesture 147; equipment 417

fair *v.* to travel, pass, 'fare'/get on 110, 258, 632; *pres.pl.* 284; **fairand** *pres.p.* 443, 588; **fure** *pt.* 8, 18, 24, 210; **farne** *pp.* 108n

fairlie *adv.* pleasantly 174

fais *see* **face**

faith *n.* faith; *phrs.* **in** ~ 'truly' (*lit.* I promise, on my faith) 226, 307, 370, 428, 488, 585, 598, 615, 707, 724, 875, 916

fall *n.* fall 152

fall *v.* to fall (in its various senses, including befall, happen, occur, descend, decline, begin) 832; *pres.pl.* 524; *pres.subj.* 60, 758; **fallis** *pres.pl.* 74; **fell (into)** *pt.* 1, 90, 726

fallow *n.* 'guy', person 54, 72, 591; more pointedly, companion or match 875

fals *adj.* false, untrue, unfaithful 500, 888

fand *see* **find**

fane *adj.* eager, happy, delighted 205, 317, 418, 615

far *see* **fer**

farthermair *adv.* further 225

fast *adv.* firmly, strongly, quickly, steadily 27, 426, 608, 701; **faster** *comp.* 547

fattest *adj.super.* as *n.pl.* the fattest ones 197

fault *n.* lack, non-performance 288

fauour *n.* favour, good will 898

fauour *v.pres.1sg.* am well-disposed (towards) 899

febill *adj.* feeble, weak 551

fecht *n.* fight, battle 874

fecht *v.* to fight, wage war 750; *pres.pl.* 524

fechting *n.* fighting, warfare 461, 873; **fechtine** 60

fee *n.* a feudal holding; *phrs.* **of** ~ with feudal rights in land 773

feid *n.* feud, enmity 506, 965

feild *n.* open land (not necessarily cultivated) 74; **feildis** *pl.* 8, 412, 443, 588

feind *n* devil 888; **feynd** 910

feir *n.* behaviour, bearing, manners 118

feir *n.* company 701n

feir *see* **in-feir**

feirslie *adv.* fiercely 18

feit *see* **fute**
feld *v.pt.* felt 97
fell *see* **fall**
fell *adj.* fierce, violent 74, 97, 730, 873
fell *n.* mountain 19; **fellis** *pl.* 2, 69
felloun *adj.* savage, fierce 910; **fellonar** *comp.* 809
fellounlie *adv.* savagely, fiercely 18
fen *n.* bog, mudpit 444
fend *v.* to defend, drive (out) 654
fensabill *adj.* militarily adept, useful in battle 327
fer *adv.* far, widely 26, 69, 346, 412, 809, 902, 910; **far** 262
ferly *adv.* wondrously, to the wonder of watchers 578
ferly *n.* wonder 402, 668; **ferlie** 899
ferlyfull *adj.* wondrous 2
fet *v.* to fetch, gather 443
few *adj.* few 588
fewaill *n.* fuel 242; **fewall** 303; **fewell** 443
fewtir *n.* lance-rest (on Rauf's saddle) 808
fy *interj.* fie! (exclamation of disgust) 873, 888
fyftene *num.* 231, 668
fylit *v.pp.* soiled 444
find *v.* to find (in its various senses, incl. discover) 61; *pres.1sg.* 427; **findis** *pres.2sg.* 240; **fand** *subj.* 70; *pt.* 72, 153, 505, 506, 507, 537, 588, 809; **found** *pp.* 288n; **fundin** 292, 500, 523, 551, 615, 762
fyne *adj.* excellent, refined 54, 679
fyre *n.* (hearth-)fire 81, 107, 109, 132, 142, 219, 222, 909
firmament *n.* the heavens 18, 289
first *adv.* first, initially 87, 759, 809
fischis *n.pl.* fish 679
fiue *num.* five 34, 654
flamand *v.pres.p.* flaming (apparently in reference to the oriflamme) 668n
flan *n.* storm 2n
fleichingis *n.pl.* flattery, insincere or cajoling speeches 898
fled *v.pt.subj.* should run away, should flee 507
flour-de-lycis *n.pl.* fleur-de-lis, the heraldic emblem of France 667
flowris *n.pl.* flowers 667
flure *n.* floor 680
folk *n.* people 19; **folkis** *pl.* 347
foly *n.* folly, foolishness 524, 552
following *v.pres.p.* following 347; **followit (to)** *pt.* 419, pertained to 506
for *conj.* because (of), on account of 56, 60, 80, 81, 87, etc.
for *prep.* appropriate to, because of 41, 45, 53, 63, 79, etc.
forbid *v.pres.subj.* prevent, forestall (it) 57, 293

forbot *n.* prohibition, act of forbidding 742
forcenes *n.* force, vigour 810; **forcynes** 816
ford *n.* (*lit.* 'ford') passage 730
forest *n.* forest (a legalism: an area subject to special jurisdiction to preserve game), wasteland 69, 195
forestaris *n.pl.* wardens appointed to preserve hunting rights 195
forfaitour *n.* forfeiture (an estate that falls to the crown owing to its holder's criminal behaviour) 759
formest *adj.super.* first 286, 578, 667, 701
forrow *prep.* ? before 537n
foroutin *prep.* without 288
forsaik *v.* to renounce, abandon 887, 937
forsuith *adv.* truly 55, 71, 146, 191, 195, 200, 302, 619, 877
forthy *adv.* therefore 371, 915
for to *prep.* (with *inf.*) to 58, 67, 232, 251, 275, etc.
forwonderit *v.pp.* mystified, perturbed 726
forwrocht *v.pp.* exhausted, overcome 834
forȝeild *v.pres.subj.* (may) repay 78
forȝet *v.* to forget 312, 965; *pp.* 125, 148
foull *adj.* dirty, poor, degrading, disgusting 432, 444, 557, 888
foullis *n.pl.* birds 523, 679
foundis *v.pres.3sg.* passes (forward) 174, 810; **foundit** *pt.* 701
foundit *v.pt.*[2] founded, established 967
fra *prep.* (away) from (including uses marking inception of an action, i.e., beginning with) 4n, 18, 33, 162, 249, etc.; *phrs.* **him fra** beside him 799
frane *v.* to inquire, ask 225
fre *adj.* unfettered, unconditional 759
freik *n.* man, warrior 615; **freikis** *pl.* 654
freind *n.* friend 226; **freindis** *pl.* 949
freindly *adv.* in a friendly way 279
freindschip *n.* friendship, amity 61
freschlie *adv.* afresh, anew, course by course 210
freuch *adj.* weak, frail 523
fry *n.* young fish 679
fryth *n.* woodlands 679
frostis *n.pl.* freezing weather 730
fule *n.* fool 507
full *adv.* very, completely, truly 26, 106, 188, 210, 222, 408, 420, 448, 456, 466, 468, 470, 474, 485, 521, 548, 570, 585, 588, 599, 602, 636, 640, 664, 666, 678, 680, 746, 791, 792, 818, 840, 901, 915, 917, 942, 945
fulfill *v.* to perform, fulfil 387, 452, 542
fundin *see* **find**
fure *see* **fair** *v.*

furth *adv.* forward or out, away (from here) 69, 262, 291, 600, 654, 862; along 397

fusioun *n.* plenty; *phrs.* **into** ~ in great plenty 210

fute *n.* foot 19, 547, 578, 816; **feit** *pl.* 444

ga *v.* to go, pass (the pp. regularly with 'be', not 'have') 423, 749; *imper.* 116, 157; **gais** *pres.pl.* 219; **gane** *pp.* 158, 238, 262, 349, 573, 627; *see also* **wend, went**

gaddering *n.* gathering 336

gay *adj.* attractive, sporty 476; **gayest** *super.* 482; as *n.* sporty man (Roland) 782

gay *adv.* gaily, pleasantly 666

gaif *v.* to give (up), surrender 498 (for **geif**); **gif** 309, 769; *pres.1sg.* 750; **geif** *pres.1sg.* 610; **gaif** *pt.* 369, 390, 835; **gaue** 649, 857, 955; *phrs.* **gif the** commit yourself ? 309n; **ane gift heir I geif** I swear (to you), assure (you) 610n

gaylie *adv.* splendidly 456

gaist *n.* guest, alien or intruder 96, 104, 108, 213; **gest** 201, 781

gaist *n.* spirit; *phrs.* **gaif the** ~ gave up the ghost, died 835

gait *n.* way, path 42, 93, 108, 782; **gaitis** *pl.* 567, 609

galȝart *adj.* valiant, hardy 781

game *n.* entertainment 952

ganandest *adj.super.* most fitting, most convenient 782

gane *adj.* direct 609

gang *v.* to go 147 ('go ahead/first'), 261, 923; *imper.* 145, 158, 487, 630; *pres.subj.* 381; **gangis** *pres.2sg.* 609; *pres.3sg.* 626; **gangand** *pres.p.* 445

gar *v.imper.* to cause, make or force 213, 396, 501, 722; **gart** *pt.* 582, 770, 860, 954

gat *see* **get**

gaue *see* **gaif**

gawin *n.* gain, benefit 381n

gedling *n.* fellow 609n, 618

geif *see* **gaif**

geir *n.* gear, equipment 482, 769

gentill *adj.* noble, well-born 182, 203, 337, 343, 570, 868, 926

gentrise *n.* nobility; *phrs.* **to do ȝow in his** ~ to place yourself at the mercy of one of his rank 368

gest *see* **gaist**

gestning *n.* entertainment as a guest 971

get *v.* to get, obtain, receive, provide, pass 445, 736; **gat** *pt.* 600, 696, 697, 702, 776, 959

gyde *n.* garment, apparel 716

gif *conj.* if 62, 110, 124, 125, 226, etc.; ~ **that** 598, 786

gif *see* **gaif**

gift *n.* gift 610n
gyrd *v.* to strike; *phrs.* **leit ~ to** loosed a blow at 149
girth *n.* peace, treaty 835
glaid *adj.* happy, pleased 77, 117, 178
glaid *adv.* happily, willingly 600
glaid *see* **glyde**
glaidlie *adv.* joyfully, happily, graciously 193; **glaidly** 616
gle *n.* pleasure, entertainment 626, 716, 952; *phrs.* **with ~** ? pleasantly 98
glemand *v.pres.p.* gleaming, shining 666
glemis *n.pl.* gleams, sparkles 456
glyde *v.* to pass forth, go 782; **glaid** *pt.* 98, 482
glitterand *v.pres.p.* glittering, shimmering 456, 666, 716, 769
god *n.* deity generally 936
gold *n.* gold, wealth, the colour gold 455, 469, 499, 705, *935n
gouerning *n.* living, sustenance 445n
gowlis *n.* the heraldic tincture ‘gules’, i.e., red 455n, 666
grace *n.* grace, the divine gift, favour or good fortune 331, 335, 483, 498, 768, 941, 947
graceles *adj.* unhappy, useless 785
gracious *adj.* gracious, filled with or displaying grace 717, 728
graid *v.pp.* prepared 141
graipis *n.pl.* ? grippers, fastenings 469n
graith *adj.* prompt 389
grant *n.* favour, boon, agreement 76, 389
granting *n.* favour 498
grantit *v.pp.* promised 317
grassum *n.* treasure, precious objects 935
grauit *v.pp.* engraved, incised (on a shield) 455
gre *n.* triumph, victory; *phrs.* **to the ~** to win victory 483
greif *n.* grief, distress, a bad outcome 381
greif *v.pres.subj.* trouble, annoy 312
greis *n.pl.* greaves, armour for the shin 469
greit *adj.* great, large 319, 325, 334, 338, 364, 369, 402, 469, 488, 683, 697, 733
grene *n.* a scarlet dye 455n, 666
grome *n.* servant, lordly man 610, 728; **gromis** *pl.* 781
ground *n.* ground, the earth; *phrs.* **on ~** alive or lively, anywhere 482, 499, 618, 835
gude *adj.* good, proper 72, 88, 172, 176, 178, 223, 255, 261, 314, 348, 389, 660, 737, 765, 820, 915, 936, 939; *as n.* good people 170
gude *n.* benefit, honour 785
gude-wyfe *n.* the mistress of the house 98, 174, 291
gudlie *adj.* well-disposed, good-humoured 118

had *see* **haue**
haikit *v.pt.* advanced 641n
haill *adj.* whole, complete 494; unblemished, sound or fresh 409
hailsum *adj.* wholesome, delightful 672
hair *adj.* hoary, grey 419
haist *n.* haste 829
haist *v.* to hasten, speed up 547
haistelie *adv.* hastily 113; **haistely** 399, 419, 822
hald *v.* to hold, retain or be steadfast, keep, restrain, preserve, consider 251, 315, 380, 409, 447, 451, 779, 797; *pres.1sg.* 746; *imper.* 371; **haldis** *pres.2sg.* 493; **held** *pt.* 223; **haldin** *pp.* 542, 564; *phrs.* ~ **na fute** keep (their) footing 19
hale *adv.* completely 52
halely *adv.* completely 892
half *n.adj.* half 152, 494, 706
hall *n.* hall, the central gathering place in a medieval house 152, 401, 641, 658, 663, 686, 737, 752
hame *n.* (and *quasi-adv.*) home, to my/the house 71, 91, 103, 107, 233, 256, 915
hamelie *adj.* plain 112
hand *n.* the hand (e.g., as a pledge) 118, 144, 150, 157, 385, 564, 845; *pl.* 865; *phrs.* **at/to** ~ nearby, beside *66n, 339, 803; into (my) possession 759
happin *v.* to befall, to chance (upon) 330, 380; **hapnis** *pres.3sg.* 758
harbreit *v.pt.* stayed, took shelter (with) 706
harberie *n.* shelter 41, 66, 83, 240, 292; **harbery** 64, 296, 672, 970
hard *adj.* harsh 599, 812
hard *adv.* harshly, with difficulty 24, 447, 602
hard *see* **heir** *v.*
hard-harnest *pp.adj.* in protective armour 829
hardy *adj. as n.* bold or brave one 641
harnes *n.* armour, military equipment 393, 409, 574
hart *n.* heart, spirit, mind 77, 402, 482, 599, 892, 939
hartfully *adv.* sincerely 887
haue *v.* to have, possess, hold/consider 135, 158, 160, 162, 242, etc.; *imper.* 255, 892; *pres.1sg.* 80, 105, 170, 201, 230, etc.; **hes** *pres.2sg.* 81, 125, 148, 160, 161, etc.; *pres.3sg.* 108, 173, 205, 631, 741; *pres.pl.* 170, 944; **haue** 196; *pres.subj.* may have 435, 483; **had** *pt.* possessed 41, 76, 93, 134, 143 etc.; *pp.* 81; **had** *pt.subj.* 61, 119, 440, 598, 661, 689, 747; *phrs.* **haue him to** cause him to be 740
he *see* **hie**
hecht *v.* to promise 451; *pt.* 527, 540, 844; *pp.* 380, 447, 779, 797
hechtis *n.pl.* promises, duties 409
heich *see* **hie**

heid *n.pl.* heads 815
heid *n.* (their need for) heedfulness, attentiveness 830n
heill *n.* good health 564, 599
heip *n.* heap, pile; *phrs.* **weill to** ~ to a fine pinnacle, to a proper conclusion 83
heir *adv.* here 66, 72, 112, 167, 179, etc.
heir *v.* to hear 330, 375, 691; *pres.1sg.* 761, 846, 936; **hard** *pt.* heard 15, 99, 280, 437, 732, 786
held *see* **hald**
hell *n.* hell 919
help *n.* help 134
help *v.* to help 253, 302
hende *adj.* as *n.* courteous person 966
heritabilly *adv.* with the right of inheriting (a property), i.e., not a personal or lifetime grant 760
het *adj.* for **hait** 'hot' 109
heuy *adj.* distressed, oppressed 830
hew *n.* 'stuff', material 550n
hewit *v.pt.* chopped, slashed 822, 829
hy *n.* haste 277, 320, 574, 641, 761, 861, 920
hicht *n.*[1] height, full extent 494; *phrs.* **on** ~ aloud, openly, loudly, visibly 630, 683, 786; **montanis on** ~ **= montanis hie** (for rhyme) 37n
hicht *n.*[2] haste; *phrs.* **upon** ~ speedily, readily 186
hidder *adv.* hither, here, to this place 583, 708
hie *adj.* high 69, 416, 572; **heich** 19; *phrs.* **on he** loudly 211
hieway *n.* direct or main road 384
hillis *n.pl.* hills 416
himself *pron.* himself 168, 205, 422, 552; *see* **hisself**
hine *adv.* hence, from here 49, 853; **hyne** 238
hing *v.* to hang (from a gallows) 740
hynt *v.pt.* seized (and removed), shoved back 574, 695
hyre *n.* wages, reward 105
hisself *pron.* himself 625; *see* **himself**
hit *v.pt.* struck 150, 861
holtis *n.pl.* woods 419, 493
hone *n.* delay 574
hope *v.pres.1sg.* think 719, 779
hors *n.* horse, mount 58, 393; *pl.* 813, 817
hour *n.* hour 828 (dative of time)
hous *n.* house, dwelling 68, 92, 166
houerit *v.pt.* halted, waited 415
how *adv.* how 86, 525, 729, 730, 732, 739
huifis *v.pres.2sg.* halt (and wait) 493
huit *v.pt.* halted (and waited) 415n
husband *n.* peasant 596

husbandman *n.* peasant, farmer 520
husband-weid *n.* a peasant's clothes 593
ilk *demon.* each, every 137, 248, 329, 351, 404, 468, 475, 483, 665, 713, 756, 836
ilkane *demon.* each 25, *200n, 863
ill *adj.* evil *743n
ill *adv.* badly, not at all 39, 108
ill *n.* malice 53
in *adv.* within, at home, inward 94, 121, 233, 391, 480, etc.
in *prep.* in, within, into 1, 5, 9, 17, 20, etc.
in-feir *adv.* together, as a pair or group 144, 174, 347, 412, 465, 578, 667, 701; **into** ~ 218
intent *n.* intention, purpose 396, 437, 449, 727
into *prep.* in, into 209, 218, 350, 460, 533, 673; **intill** 409
inuy *n.* animosity, malice; *phrs.* **haue at** ~ express malice toward 196
inwart *adj.* intimate 236
is *see* **be**
ischar *n.* usher, door-keeper, officer responsible for precedents 643
ithand *pp.adj.* continuous, persistent 27
iwis *adv.* truly, certainly 35, 143, 161, 248, 690, 726

iewellis *n.pl.* jewels *474n
ioynit *v.pp.* assembled 694
iornay *n.* expedition, pursuit of arms 587; **iornayis** *pl.* 795
iornaying *n.* encounter, exchange of arms 483

keip *n.* attention; *phrs.* **tak** ~ pay attention (to), heed, guard attentively 637, 754
keip *v.* to preserve or retain, uphold 162, 537, 959
keipeir *n.* custodian, guardian 771
ken *v.* to know, indicate, teach or instruct, recognise 325, 446, 718; *pres.1sg.* 436, 704; *pres.pl.* 766; **kend** *pt.* 650; *pp.* 950
kendill (on) *v.imper.* light 107
kene *adj.* brave, fierce 841, 859, 962; *adv.* 871
kest *v.pt.* cast, threw, inserted, tossed about or considered (usually in the mind) 365, 402, 714, 808, 820, 838; *see* **cast**
kyith *v.imper.* show (your understanding that) 107; **kythand** *pres.p.* displaying, showing off 705
kin *n.* nature, kind of, kin or lineage 233, 358, 926; ~ **a** 591
kynd *n.* nature, type of person 126n; *phrs.* **of** ~ by the nature (of your apparent social class) 163
king *n.* king 7, 13, 30, 39, 40, 44, 53, 57, 75, 88, 117, 120, 123, 147, 149, 168, 177, 182, 194, 199, 205, 216, 223, 228, 250, 270, 273, 277, 285, 295, 306, 317, 325, 330, 332, 361, 389, 403, 420, 425, 431, 487, 498,

500, 533, 573, 579, 583, 600, 658, 702, 710, 723, 727, 732, 738, 770, 786, 902, 952, 960, 967; **kingis** *poss.* 438, 453; *poss.pl.* 718
kythand *see* **kyith**
kirk *n.* church 573
knaifis *n.pl.* serving men, grooms 113
knap *v.imper.* strike 111
knaw *v.pres.subj.* know, recognise, prove 260; **knew** *pt.subj.* 367, 558; **knawin** *pp.* 254, 379; recognised 501; familiar 532
knawledge *n.* knowledge, familiarity, experience 246, 325
kne *n.* knee(s) 337
kneillit *v.pt.* knelt 333, 421; **kneilit** 337
knicht *n.* knight 30, 337, 340n, 421, 429, 454, 491, 538, 570, 583, 736, 745, 751, 754, 772, 787, 793, 803, 841, 845, 859, 868, 872, 889, 933, 962; **knichtis** *pl.* 740, 766, 951
knichtheid *n.* knighthood 959
knyfe *n.* knife 863; **knyfis** *pl.* 865

lady *n.* mistress, wife 229
lay *v.pt.* lay (down, i.e., rested), passed 93, 278, 330, 814, 817; **laid** *pp.* laid out, offered 297; *phrs.* **layd = lay it** *v.pres.1sg.* wager it 374
laid *n.* load 245, 300, 323, 639; **laidis** *pl.* 445, 508
laid *v.pt. see* **leid**
laiser *n.* space, opportunity 565; **lasair** 631
lait *adv.* (*lit.* recently) quickly 40n
laith *adj.* hostile, indisposed (to), reluctant (to) 639, 699, 822, 832; *phrs.* **me war** ~ it would be displeasing to me 285 (*similarly* 639)
laithly *adv.* hostilely, fiercely 137
lak *v.* to criticise, deprecate 87
land *n.* land, country 47, 68, 161, 590, 917; **landis** *pl.* 927
lane *v.* to hide, conceal 313
lang *adj.* (over)extensive, extended, tedious 277, 827
lap *see* **leip**
last *n. phrs.* **at the** ~ in this extremity, ultimately 31, 225
lat *v.* to let, allow 832, 856n; *imper.* 212, 291, 377, 525, 616, 622; **leit** *pt.* allowed, permitted, caused 149, 629; **lattin** *pp.* 612; *phrs.* ~ **be** stop, on no account 293
laubour *n.* honest work 509
lauch *v.* to laugh 783; **leuch** *pt.* 519, 738
lauchfull *adj.* law-abiding 508
lawtie *n.* loyalty, fidelity 509, 601
left *see* **leif**
leid *n.* people (but perhaps just ‘man’) 395n, 590
leid *v.* to lead, pursue, carry on, carry or transport 508; *pres.1sg.* 47; **leidis** 50; **led** *pt.* 263; *pp.* handled 739; **laid** *pt.* brought, spread 137; **leidand** *pres.p.* 594

leif *n.* leave 279, 318, 555
leif *v.*[1] to leave (off) (in its various senses), abandon, stop 172, 423, 612, 784, 822; *pres.1sg.* 639; *imper.* 65; **left** *pt.* 571, 816
leif *v.*[2] to believe 940
leif *v.*[3] to live 950, 966n; **lyfe** 856; **leifis** *pres.3sg.* 509; **leuand** *pres.p.* living 784, 918
leill *adj.* true, just, faithful 601
leip (on) *v.* to mount (a horse) 85; **lap** *pt.* 277
leird *v.pp.* taught, instructed 169
leis *v.imper.* lose 640
leit *see* **lat**
lelely *adv.* truthfully 311, 940
lely *n.* lily 671
lemit (vp) *v.pt.* brightened, shone 324
len *v.* to give or grant 331
lent *v.pp.* passing 395, 590
lenth *n.* 'length', space 860
lesing *n.* lie, deception 310
lest *v.* to last 783
let *n.* hindrance, delay 144, 318, 539
let *v.* to delay 306
letting n. delay 424
leuch *see* **lauch**
leuand *see* **leif**
licht *adj.*[1] bright 324
licht *adj.*[2], *adv.* easy 634; *adv.phrs.* **set bot/at sa** ~ think of small consequence or value, hold in contempt 739, 935
licht *n.* (day)light 837
lichtly *adv.* frivolously, derisively 519
liddernes *n.* depravity, cowardice 784
lie *v.* to lie (tell an untruth) 846
lyfe *n.* life, mode of living 168, 169, 277, 374, 376, 433, 743, 783; **life** 47; **lyfis** *poss.* 949; *phrs.* **on lyfe** alive, living 590
lyfe *v. see* **leif**
lyft *n.* sky 324
lyis *v.pres.3sg.* lies, is currently resident 246, 723
lyke *adj.* likely 519
lyking *n.* pleasure, desire 856
lykis *v. impers. pres.3sg.* it pleases him (to) 612, 946; **lykit** *pt.* (with **ill**) it displeased the king 39; **lykand** *pres.p.* (with **euill**) it was displeasing to the king 40
ling *n.*[1] heather (for 'the moor' more generally) 395
ling *n.*[2] line; *phrs.* **in a** ~ directly, quickly 426
lystinit *v.pt.* listened 738

lytill *adj.* little (space), small 57, 80, 799
lofe *v.* to praise 87
loft *n.* the sky; *phrs.* **vpon** ~ either on high (at high table) or loudly 738, 783
lois *v.* to lose 639
lord *n.* lord, master, God 128, 349, 726, 783, 940; **lordis** *pl.* 738, 752
lorne *v.pp.* lost 433
loud *adv.* audibly; *phrs.* **on** ~ aloud 846
ludgeit *v.pp.* given lodging 739
lufe *n.* love 45, 856
lufesumly *adv.* courteously 556
luke *v.* to see, look 723; **lukit** *pt.* 799

ma *adj.* more in number 327, 328, 427 (i.e., no more intruders), 668, 747
mad *adj.* witless, simple, *or representing* **ma(i)t** *adj.* exhausted 441n
madlie *adv.* like mad men 22
magre *n.* hostility 485
may *v.pres.* may (in various senses, basically have the power to) 209, 252, 253, 301, 302, 304, 316, 371, 380, 446, 494, 511, 543, 646, 719, 736, 783, 849, 910, 938; ?controls 884; *see* **micht**, **mocht**
maid *see* **mak**
maiden *n.* the blessed Virgin 510
mair *adj.comp.* more, the greater, further 61, 162, 172, 318, 415, 503, 691, 707, 837, 921; *adv.* further 270, 511, 553; **(the) mair** *quasi-n.* a greater (part) 309; *phrs.* **withoutin ony** ~ with no delay, immediately 149; **but** ~ with no delay, although conceivably without any more (an ironic comment on great ceremony for a small company) 184
maist *adj.super.* most, greatest, biggest 68, 171, 230, 236, 360, 391, 801, 884; principal, primary 227
maisterfull *adj.* overbearing, violent 442
mait *adj.* overcome, exhausted 831; *see* **mad**
mak *v.* to make (in its various senses, incl. force or coerce, agree) 128, 172, 310, 321, 755 (1st use), etc.; *pres.1sg.* 755 (2nd use); *imper.* 300, 881; **makis** *pres.2sg.* 95; **mak** *pres.pl.* 200; **maid** *pt.* 121, 178, 220, 510, 728, etc.; *pp.* 77, 319n, 484, 602, 745, etc.; *phrs.* **why makis thou no dule** why don't you display sorrow 95; **maid a strange fair** behaved strangely 147; **maid thame eis** settled down comfortably 220
maker *n.* creator 893
man *n.* man 12, 67, 138, 287, 312, 355, 367, 372, 391, 397, 404, 441, 484, 504, 508, 541, 546, 589, 592, 599, 617, 637, 650, 659, 721, 744, 746, 755, 768, 801, 953; adult 361; **men** *pl.* 20, 327, 442, 546, 829, 833, 871, 886, 943; *indef.pron.* folks, people 46
manassing *n.* threats 200
mane *adj.* great(est); *phrs.* **Charlis the Mane** Charles the great (a calque on Fr. 'Charles le grand/magne' or Lat. 'Carolus magnus') 203

manly *adj.* courageous, valiant 484, 755
mantene *v.* to support, sustain 849
mar *see* **mer**
mary *interj.* an oath of surprise, 'by the Virgin' 57, 367
marschell *n.* marshal 961
marschellit *v.pp.* arranged in order, placed at table 184
matche *v.* associate (with), rival 442; **matchit** *pp.* made tablemates 184
meiknes *n.* meekness, humility 652
meit *n.* food, dinner 81, 660
meit *v.* to meet, encounter 527, 563, 793; **meitis** *pres.pl.* 250; *pres.2sg.* (*subj.)* 395; **met** *pt.* 138, 606, 729, 734, 967; *pp.* 440, 441, 848
mekle *adj.* much, great 6, 47, 460, 509, 514, 884, 921; **mekill** 61, 338; *adv.* more 138
men *see* **man**
mend *v.* to improve, restore 652, 953
mene *v.* to intend; *phrs.* **maid him to** ~ acted as if he intended 121
menstrallis *n.pl.* minstrels 355
mer *v.* to become confused, go astray 22; **mar** *v.pres.subj.* hinder 511
mercy *n.* mercy 941
merwell *n.* wonder 514
mes *n.* mass 572
message *n.* envoy, messenger 904
mesure *n.* moderation 652
met *see* **meit**
metaill *n.* metal 826
meting *n.* meeting, (armed) encounter 335, 485
micht *n.* might, power 182, 338, 755, 849, 937; **michtis** *pl.* 884; *phrs.* **Charlis of micht** Charles the powerful (a calque on Fr. 'Charles le grand/magne' or Lat. 'Carolus magnus') 182
micht *v.pt.* had power to (do s.t.) 19, 155, 479, 652, 654; *subj.* 83, 84, 110, 330, 497, 720, 810; *see* **may**, **mocht**
michtie *adj.* powerful, valiant 485
midmorne *n.* the middle of the morning 29, 415
mylis *n.pl.* miles 49; *pl.poss.* miles' 34
myrk *adj.* dark 22
mirrie *adj.* joyous 135
mirthfull *adj.* filled with joy, joyful 355, 953
mirthis *n.pl.* joy, happiness 953
myself *pron.reflex.* I, me 58, 236, 303, 631; *see* **self**
myster *n.* skill, art, need 442, 747
mocht *v.pt.* had power (to) 268, 384, 490, 913 (*always in rhyme*); *see* **may**, **micht**
mon *v.pres.* must (go) 425, 691
mony *adj.* many (a) 3, 6, 12, 17, 161, 221, 275, 328, 340, 353, 356, 430,

444, 446, 461, 521, 533, 573, 659, 668, 694, 697, 713, 728, 751, 927, 944, 953, 962

montane *n.* mountain 792; **montanis** *pl.* 22, 35, 37

morne *n.* morning, dawn 272, 322, 363, 431, 777; *phrs.* **the** ~ tomorrow (dative of time) 286, 299, 304, 312

morning *n.* morning 9, 85, 393

mot *v.pres.* may 53, 129, 285

mother *n.* mother, the Blessed Virgin 495, 510

mure *n.* moor 14, 563, 734

na *adv.conj.* no, none, nor 19 (2x), 30, 31, 41, 66, etc.; *see* **nane**

nabody *n.* no one 34

nay *n.* denial; *phrs.* **that is na** ~ no one could deny it 688

nait *n.* advantage, usefulness 61

name *n.* name 45, 63, 239, 255, 311, 314, 650, 872, 907, 913, 969

namit *v.pt.* named 503

nane *adj.* no, none (usually preceding a vowel) 53, 82, 376, 507, 535, 545, 876; *num.pron.* none, not a single one, nothing 21, 68, 160, 172, 191, 261, 266, 653, 930; *see* **na**

nanis *adv.* nonce, occasion; *phrs.* **for the** ~ appropriate to the occasion (but often only emptily assertive 'truly') 469, 687

nathing *n.* nothing 411, 506, 560

neid *v.pres.1sg.* need, require 545

neidlingis *adv.* of necessity, necessarily 405

neir *adv.* nearly, nearby 91, 346, 412, 798, 840, 867; *adj.* near *66n; *prep.* next to 177

nek *n.* the neck 123

neuer *adv.* never 97, 99, 136, 153, 168, 228, 309, 392, 428, 538, 783, 847, 853, 878, 909, 923

new *v.* to renew 544

newlingis *adv.* recently, lately 961

nicht *n.* night 38, 83, 135, 184, 262, 328, 431, 743, 776; *pl.* 960; **nichtis** *poss.* 296

nichtit *v.impers.pt.* he was benighted, was overtaken by night 40

nyne *num.* nine 960

nyse *adj.* vain, haughty 428n

nixt *adj.* next 757, 900

nobill *adj.* noble, splendid 54, 702

nobilnes *n.* nobility, wealth 688

nocht *adv.* not 56, 270, 284, 306, 446, 766, 824; **not** 65, 79, 286, 301, 313, 367, 373, etc.

nocht *n.* nothing 789, 894, 895, 993; **not** 202, 431, 651; *phrs.* **of/for** ~ of no avail, worth nothing 491, 907

noy *n.* irritation, vexation 535

none *n.* 'nones', midday, lunchtime 282, 342, 400, 545, 576
nor *conj.* nor (often following co-ordinating **nouther**) 81, 82, 412, 431, 450, 503, 504, 652, 935; than 545
not *see* **nocht**
nouther *conj.* neither (completed by...**nor**) 81, 412, 431, 450
now *adv.* now 126, 148, 311, 537, 630, 733, 842, 846, 848, 852, 898, 899
nurtour *n.* training, proper manners 160

obeysand *adj.* obedient, subservient 124
ocht *n.* anything (at all), at all, any possible profit 253, 302, 371, 490, 644, 899; *adv.* any 553
of *prep.* out of, from (among) 5, 13, 17, 23, 27, etc.
of *adv.* off 172, 574
office *n.* an assigned duty, the position responsible for carrying it out 230, 233, 287
officiaris *n.pl.* officials, individuals with specific (household) duties 254
oft *adv.* often, frequently 430, 444, 523, 896, 945; **ofter** *comp.* 643
oft-tymes *adv.* frequently 170, 636
on *adv.* upon, onward, away 27, 85 (2nd use), 107, 202, 277, etc.
on *prep.* on 19, 37, 74, 85 (1st use), 133, etc.
ony *adj.* any 60, 72, 149, 312, 316, 318, 395, 397, 511, 617, 736, 795
onwart *n.* an earnest, advance payment 244
or *conj.*[1] before 92, 249, 291, 433, 719, 821; ~ **that** 628
or *conj.*[2] or 124, 245, 330, 381, 432, etc.
ordanit *v.pt.* organised, prepared, disposed 323, 329
ordour *n.* order (of knighthood) 754
outragious *adj.* excessive, too great 369
outray *n.* injury, hurt 156, 876
outrayd *v.pt.* treated violently, abused 372
outwart *adv.* outward, toward the edges 329, 604
outwith *prep.* outside of 410
ouir *adv*. above 473
ouir *prep*. over, above, on top of, throughout 8, 14, 328 (post-posited), 382, 445, etc.; *adv*. more than 49
ouir-airlie *adv.* too soon 79
ouirall *adv*. completely, over the whole surface 682
ouir-hie *adj.* excessively tall 806

pay *n.* payment 297, 298
pay v. to please, pay or reward 291; **payit** *pp.* pleased, satisfied 70, 579
paintit *v.pp.* painted, decorated 663
palfray *n.* charger 276
palys *n.* palace 354; **palice** 614
pane *n.* a rich cloth; *phrs.* **in** ~ richly attired, in rich attire 5, 234, 623

pardie *interj.* by God 166, 530
pardoun *n.* remission of sins, legal pardon 921
parische *v.* to die 20
part *n.* portion, side (in a dispute), share 56, 832; *phrs.* **twa** ~ partly, mainly (*lit.* two parts of three) 123
parting *n.* departure 86
partit *v.pt.* separated 569
pas *v.* to pass, go, travel 71; *pres.pl.* 341, 567; *imper.* 622; **past** *pt.* 5, 833; *pp.* 29 ('had passed'); *phrs.* **out of the renk past** withdrew from the field of combat
passage *n.* the way 416
pauyot *n.* page 276
peir *n.* peer, match 663; *phrs.* **of that ilk** ~ closely similar, their true match 468
perpetuallie *adv.* in perpetuity 938; **perpetually** 968
picht *v.pp.* 'pitched', set, encrusted 467
pithis *n.pl.* (respective) strengths, vigour 862
place *n.* place 333, 854, 967
playis *v.pres.pl.* play (musical instruments) 355
plaitis *n.pl.* the metal plates comprising a suit of armour 467
plane *adj.* flat, level, open 416
plane *adv.* plainly, openly 315
plane *n.* ground 613
plentie *n.* abundance 207, 358
plesance *n.* pleasure 358; *phrs.* **withoutin** ~ angrily, discourteously 906
plesand *adj.* pleasing, pleasant 623
plicht *v.pres.1sg.* pledge, swear 939
point *n.* point; *phrs.* **in ~...to** on the verge of 20
porter *n.* porter, door-keeper 622
porter-swayne *n.* door-keeping servant 606
power *n.* power; *phrs.* **in** ~ sufficiently strong 885
pray *v.pres.1sg.* ask, request, beseech, plead 59, 306, 591, 646, 882; *pres. pl.* 331; **prayit** *pt.* 282; **prayd** *pp.* 879
precious *adj.* precious 467
preichand *v.pres.pl.* asserting, exhorting 345
preif *v.* to put (it) to the test, prove (at law) 304, 314, 614; **preifit** *pp.* 497; *see* **prufe**
preikit *v.pt.* rode 408
preis *n.* a throng or company 623
preis *v.pres.pl.* press, advance, strain 862; **preisses** *v.pres.3sg.* 614
preistis *n.pl.* priests 344
preiudice *n.* (preconceived) hostility or enmity 497
prelat *n.* a 'lord of the church' (normally a bishop or head of a monastic house) 353; **prelatis** *pl.* 6

presoun *n.* prisoner 885
prest *adj*. ready (for action) 468; *adv.* readily, eagerly 408
preuie *adj.* private 263
preuilie *adv.* quietly, unobtrusively 276, 710
price *n.* honour, renown, prowess 832
pryde *n.* pomp, splendour 6
pryme *n.* the first (ecclesiastical) hour, early morning 23
principall *adj.* great, considerable 358
princis *n.pl.* great lords 6, 350
pryse *v.imper.* appraise, assess 86; **prys** 252
processioun *n.* an ecclesiastical procession 345
profferit *v.pt.* offered (to allow) 147
profite *n.* profit (both material and spiritual) 921
properlie *adv*. appropriately 467; **properly** 663, 862
prophecie *n.* prophecy, here specifically the Old Law promises of Jesus's birth 345
proud *adj.* resplendent, outstanding 352; **proudest** *super.* 5, 20, 234; as *n.* most resplendent people 5, 623
proudly *adv.* in a noble manner, with magnificence or majesty 408
prufe *v.* to put to the test, demonstrate 862; *see* **preif**
pulanis *n.pl.* pieces of armour covering the knees 468
pund *n.* pounds' worth (of income from property) 756
pure *adj.* faultless (or poor, miserable?) 20n
put *v.* place 121; *pt.* 119; *pres.subj.* 539

quemely *adv.* closely, neatly 681
quene *n.* 229, 234, 250, 528, 531, 715
quha *pron.* whoever, anyone who 912
quhair *adv.conj.* where, to a place where 3, 34, 75, 93, 131, etc.
quhaireuer *adv.* wherever 240
quhairsaeuer *pron.* wherever 758
quhasa *pron.* whoever 674
quhat *pron.adj.* which, what 30, 233, 238, 311, 364, 403, 498, 502, 591, 691
quhatsa *pron.* whatever 511
quhatsumeuer *pron.* whatever sort (of person), whoever 398
quhen *adv.conj.* when(ever) 55, 85, 120, 139, 176, etc.
quhy *adv.* why 95, 596
quhiddersa *adv.* whichever way (of two), however 381
quhill *conj.prep.* until 91, 151, 154, 225, 283, etc.; *conj*. while, so long as 141, 290. 543, 783, 918; (to the point) that, so that 655
quhip *n.* whip 385
quhome *pron.* whomever 505
quoke *v.pt.* trembled, grimaced 731

raid *see* **ryde**
raifand *v.pres.p.adj.* (lit. raving, mad) incomprehensible 648
raik *v.* to pass, move 212; *pres.subj.* 548
rais *v.* to deface, cut or slash 549
rais *v.pt.* arose 215
raith *adv.* quickly 548, 607, 818
ran *v.pt.* ran 819, 869
rauingis *n.pl.* nonsense, extravagant speeches 894
realme *n.* realm, kingdom 925
record *n.* account, tale 728
reddy *adj.* prepared 321, 762; likely 58
reddyit *v.pt. (refl.)* made himself ready 778, 807
regaird *n.* attention; *phrs.* **at** ~ in their consideration 651; *see* **rewaird**
reid *n.* red 669
rek *v.pres.1sg.* care (about), take heed (of) 894, 933; **rekkis** *pres.pl.* 895
remeid *n.* remedy (against sin) 510
remufe *v.* to withdraw, retreat 860
renk *n.* 'rank', line or path, space of a jousting run 548, 808, 833
renkis *n.pl.* warriors 818
rent *v.pp.* torn, wounded 834
repreif *v.pres.1sg.* rebuke, find fault with 842n
ressonabill *adj.* just, equitable 757n
ressoun *n.* reason, reasonable or appropriate behaviour 119, 214, 259; **resoun** 883; *phrs.* **with** ~ reasonably 84; **be** ~ as a consequence 252, 925; **out of** ~ unreasonably, discourteously 378
rest *n.* resting place, shelter 59n
rest *v.* to rest 404, 777
restles *adj.* active 818, 833
retinew *n.* a knight's 'following', his troop or household 774
return *v.* to return 290
reulit *v.pp.* regulated, arranged or decorated (in a linear or band-like pattern?) 466n, 669, 670, 685
reuall n. a wheel-shaped design, ? with an encircling border 669n
reuerence *n.* respect, deference 895
reuest *v.pp.* clothed in full ecclesiastical garb 344
rew *n.* street, inhabitants of a street 351
rew *v.* to regret, lament 548
rewaird *n.* regard, attention, recompense 959; *phrs.* **he gaue na** ~ he paid no attention 649; *see* **regaird**
ryall *adj.* noble, royal, regal 109, 480, 481, 549, 778, 791, 934; **ryallest** *super.* 478; *as n.* regal man 14
ryallie *adv.* royally, in a noble fashion 351; **ryally** 670
ryaltie *n.* royalty, dignity, pomp, magnificence 687

riche *adj.* rich, costly, powerful, many (a) 465, 673, 818, 833, 922, 927; **richest** *super.* 575; as *n.pl.* rich men 925
riches *n.* riches, wealth; *phrs.* **with** ~ richly 351, 933
richt *adj.* proper, correct 45, 239, 311; the right side 150; *adv.* properly, exactly, directly, very, much too 466, 475, 579, 585, 791, 848, 868, 962, 963
richt *n.* just behaviour, legal right (esp. that of holding an estate or real property) 757n, 843; *phrs.* **at all** ~ in every way proper 685; *phrs.* **in** ~ in their legal holding 966
richt *v.* to construct, prepare 770n
rid *n.* 'rede', counsel 259
rid *v.pres.1sg.* advise, counsel 284, 435, 887
ryde *v.* to ride 479, 778; *pres.pl.* 291; **rydis** *pres.3sg.* 791; **rydand** *pres.p.* 326, 570, 807, 868; **raid** *pt.* 14, 30, 75, 480, 585
ryfe *adj.* abundant, plentiful 170
ring *n.* ring 958
rob *n.* robe 575
rois *n.* the rose 670
ronsy *see* **runsy**
roustie *adj.* rust-covered, worn out or disused 518
rowme *n.* space 808
rubeis *n.pl.* rubies 465
rude *adj.* rough, wild, uncultivated 14, 790, 934
rude *n.* Christ's cross 259, 549, 842; *poss.sg.* of the cross 45
rude-braid *n.* 'furrow-breadth', a rod (16½ feet) 860
rufe *adj.* strong, powerful 109n
rufe *n.* roof, ceiling 669
runsy *n.* riding horse 790, 869; **ronsy** 479
ruschit *v.pt.* moved quickly 790, 818, 861, 869
ruse *v.* to praise 80; **rusit** *pt.* 481

sa *adv. conj.* so, thus, then, as a result 8, 18 (2x), 22, 24, 27, etc.; **swa** 56; **sa that** on the condition that 751
sacramentis *n.pl.* sacraments 955
sadill *n.* saddle 475
sadly *adv.* steadfastly, persistently 655
say *n.* saw, story 732
say *v.* 99, 248, 378, 644, 719, 732, 886, 936; *pres.subj.* 236; *pres.pl.* 89, 198; *imper.* 624; **sayis** *pres.2sg.* 851; *pres.3sg.* 46, 192, 353, 870; **said** *pt.* 53, 55, 57, 88, 103, etc.; *pp.* 315; **sayand** *pres.p.* 77
saif *adv.* saving, except for 589
saik *n.* behalf; *phrs.* **for his/my** ~ on his/my account 110, 243
saill *n.*[1] sale, business 243
saill *n.*[2] hall 712

sair *adv.* grievously, painfully 636, 709
saird *v.pt.* injured 655
sall *v.pres.* shall, will *the usual form marking the future* 85, 122, 159, 198, 201, 238, etc.; **sal** *the form when followed by* **be** 56, 308, 433, 551, 745 (*without* **be** 238); **suld** *pres.subj.* should, ought, be obligated to 71, 124, 158, 162, 163, etc.
salust *v.pt.* saluted, greeted 422
same *adj.* same, this very 847
sapheir *n.(pl.)* sapphire(s) 464
sanct *n.* saint: *see Index of Proper Names*
sat *see* **sit**
saue *v.pres.subj.* save 500
saw *see* **se**
scant *n.* scarcity, an insufficient number 273
schame *n.* shame (*and quasi-adj.* shameful) 87, 488, 897n
schame *v.* to be ashamed, i.e., be backward about showing 301
schapin *v.pp.* shaped, formed, decked out 459
scheild *n.* shield 459
schene *adj.* beautiful 459, 942
schent *v.pp.* shamed, injured, lost 731
schill *adj.* cold, chilly 59
schynand *v.pres.p.* shining 470; *adj.* resplendent 558
schir *n.* sir (both polite address and as title) 45, 78, 89, 103, 159, etc.; *see* **syre**
scho *pron.* she 99 (2x), 103, 251, 931
schone *n.pl.* shoes (equivalent to 'winning one's spurs') 764n
schord *v.pp.* threatened 732
schort *adj.* short 863
schroud *v.pp.* adorned, arrayed 459
schow *n.* shove, push 697
scorne *n.* insult, act of derision 557
scorne *v.* to ridicule, deride 429
scorning *n.* ridicule 436
se *v.* to see (in its various senses, incl. show, demonstrate, look after, heed) 305, 375, 498, 525, 601, 804, 810n; **sene** 676; **se** *pres.1sg.* 289, 554, 870; *imper.* 306, 640, 753n; *pres.pl.* 343; *pres.subj.* 400; **seis** *pres.2sg.* 202, 397, 559; **saw** *v.pt.* 31, 332, 411, 417, 515, 600, 652, 711, 800, 840, 847; **sene** *pp.* seen, visible, evident, perceived (as) 357, 461, 662, 802, 875, 943
sechand *see* **seik**
seiges *n.pl.* warriors 712
seik *v.* to seek or search for, travel or advance 625, 630, 635; **sechand** *pres.p.* 506; **socht** *pt.* 388, 655, 897; *pp.* 661
seir *adj.* various, different 25, 567, 713, 922, 955; *adv.* variously 665; *phrs.* **in** ~ variously, abundantly 677

selcouthly *adv.* marvellously, wondrously 677
self *n.* self; *phrs.* **my...~** 635; *see* **myself**
self-willit *pp.adj.* obstinate, stubborn 908
sell *v.* to sell 50, 252, 302, 305
semblay *n.* assembly, gathering, celebration 357; **semblie** 662
semblit *v.pt.* assembled, gathered, passed (into) 589
semelie *adv.* beautifully 459; **semely** 665; *adj.* 676, 712
semis *v.pres.2sg.* seem, appear 54, 753; **him** ~ *pres.3sg.impers.* (it) accords with him, he appears 744; **semit** *pt.* 805, 809
sen *conj.* since 51, 127, 214, 298, 361, etc.; ~ **that** 565
send *v.pp.* sent 251; *pt.* 947; **sent** 966
senȝeorabill *adj.* noble, worthy to be a(n over)lord 713
serue *v.* to serve (in its various senses, incl. to honour, be of use), deserve 67, 268, 406; **seruis** *pres.3sg.* 907n; **seruit** *pp.* 80, 181, 712, 741
seruice *n.* service, duty to a superior, a church service 352, 636
sesit *v.pp.* seised, invested, given owner- and lord-ship 921
set *v.* to place, set or adorn (with), establish, undertake, account, set upon or be beset 392; *pres.1sg.* 634, 935; *pp.* 181, 447, 475, 665, 677, 735, 739
seuin *num.* seven 49, 661, 724
sextie *num.* sixty 773
sib-men *n.pl.* kinsmen 897
sic *adj.* such 33, 67, 70, 90, 140, etc.; *phrs.* ~ **ten** ten alike, ten just like you 329, 440
sicht *n.* sight 589, 661, 702, 847, 870; opinion 741; *phrs.* **at ane** ~ visible all at once 344
syde *n.* side, piece or detail, direction, party (in a dispute) 8, 183, 248, 289, 475, 665, 713, 836
siluer *n.* silver 676
simpill *adj.* of low rank, humble, common 164, 373, 767
sin *n.* sin 920
sindrie *adv.* apart 29; *adj.* various, different 221
syne *adv.* afterwards, next 87, 183, 189, 213, 218, etc.
syre *n.* lordly man 713; *see* **schir**
sit *v.* to sit (idly) 99; **sat** *pt.* 177, 183
skaith *n.* harm, damage 820
skill *n.* reason; *phrs.* **war bot lytill** ~ would be quite unreasonable 57
slais *v.pres.3sg.* kills, destroys 746; **slane** *pp.* 896
smylit *v.pt.* smiled 710
sobernes *n.* moderation, reasonableness 525
socht *see* **seik**
solempnit *v.pp.adj.* hallowed or sanctified, blessed through ritual, ceremonial 404, 662
sone *adv.* immediately, quickly 142, 273, 281, 332, 570, 702, 807, 848, 863
sone *n.* son 356, 942, 947

soudanis *n,pl.* sultans, Muslim rulers 897
sour *adj.* (of wood) green, unseasoned 909
souerance *n.* safety or immunity, a truce 879
space *n.* period of time 334
spair *v.imper.* stint, save up, grant mercy 202; **spaird** *pt.* 653
spak *v.pt.* spoke 270, 279, 378
spedely *adv.* with haste 653
speid *v.imper.* hasten 426; **sped** *pt.* 653
speir *v.* to ask, inquire 581; *imper.* 256; *pres.1sg.* 53; **speiris** *v.pres.2sg.* 51
speiris *n.pl.* spears 814
spend *v.imper.* expend, use 202
splenders *n.pl.* splinters 814
sperpellit *v.pt.* scattered, dispersed 26
sprent *v.pt.* sprang or leapt 811, 815
springis *n.pl.* spring-time, campaign-season 900
spuilȝe *v.* plunder, despoil 900
spurris *n.pl.* spurs 811
squyar *n.* squire 771; **squyaris** *pl.* 773
squyary *n.* a body of attendants 273
squechonis *n.pl.* scutcheons, blazons 683
stabill *n.* stable 116
stad *v.pp.* placed, exposed 136, 602
stait *n.* estate, social standing or rank 706
stakkerit *v.pt.* staggered 151, 859
stalwart *adj.* courageous, bold 698, 744, 874
staluartlie *adv.* resolutely, courageously 32
stand *v.* to stand (up or firmly), stop still or hesitate 120, 155; *pres.pl.* 864; **stude** *pt.* 454
stanis *n.pl.* gemstones 463, 467
start *n.* instant, brief space 891
start *v.pt.* leapt (up) 155, 281
steid *n.*[1] steed, horse 32, 477, 811, 963
steid *n.*[2] place, position or office 673, 859, 963
steill *n.* steel 471, 772
steill *v.* to steal or slink off 603
steir *n.* in *phrs.* **on** ~ astir, stirring 411
steiris *v.pres.3sg.* stirs, goes his way 12; **steird** *pp.* moved, disturbed 173
stiflie *adv.* firmly, vigorously 16; **stifly** 864
stynt *v.* to stop, leave off 699
stonischit *v.pp.* dismayed, astonished 173
storme *n.* storm 32; **stormis** *pl.* 136
stound *n.* (*lit.* period of time) (at this) hour 619
stour *n.* onslaught, battle 602, 864
stout *adj.* strong, bold 12, 477, 744, 772, 874

stoutly *adv.* strongly, boldly 155, 520
stray *n.* wandering; *phrs.* **on** ~ in his charge 477
straid *v.pt.* walked on 32
straik *n.* stroke, blow 173, 817
straik *see* **stryke**
strait *adj.* narrow, constrained or constraining 730
strang *adj.* strong 874
strange *adj.* strange 147
stranger *n.* stranger 214
stryfe *n.* dissension, trouble 172
stryke *v.* to contend, give a blow, pierce 520; **straik** *pt.* 811; **strikin** *pp.* 817
stryking *n.* dealing blows 744
striue *v.* to contend, dispute 553
stubill *adj.* rough, rustic 520
stude *see* **stand**
sture *adj.* strong, sturdy 817; *adv.* powerfully, violently *16n
sturely *adv.* with violence, violently 859
succourit *v.pt.* saved, preserved 743
succuderus *adj.* proud, arrogant 908
succudrously *adv.* proudly, arrogantly 855
suddand *adj.* unforeseen, intrusive 539
suddandly *adv.* suddenly, unforeseenly 735
suith *n.* truth 52, 89, 248, 378, 379, 732
sum *adj.* some, a certain 56, 59, 61, 64, 539, 655, 886; *n.* a portion 303
summoundis *n.* an order (to appear); *phrs.* **sit** ~ ignore a command 99
sumtyme *adv.* on past occasions 206
supper *n.* supper 133, 141, 142, 354; **suppar** 181; **suppair** 221
suppois *conj.* although 766
suppois *v.pres.1sg.* believe, expect 257
suttelly *adv.* cunningly, wondrously, with great craft 677
swa *see* **sa**
sweit *adj.* sweet, loving 947
swet *v.pt.* engaged (in a behaviour), sought favour 636n
swyftlie *adv.* immediately 948
swyith *adv.* quickly 116, 622; **swyth** 486
swoir *v.pt.* swore 948; **sworne** *pp.* 435
swordis *n.pl.* swords 819, 826, 948

ta *v.* 565; *imper.* take (in its various senses, incl. give or commit [oneself], receive) 114; **tak** 144, 157, 279, 314, 393, 637, 754, 837, 937; **takis** *pres.2sg.* 876; **tuke** *pt.* 118, 318, 556; **tuik** 25, 845; **tane** *pp.* 156, 240
taillis *n.pl.* conversation, stories 140, 221, 560
taist *v.imper.* test, make trial *55n
takin *n.* emblem, symbol 457

tald *see* **tell**
talk *n.* conversation 90
tane *see* **ane**
tauld *see* **tell**
teind *n.* one-tenth 474
teir *adj.* difficult 474
tell *v.* to tell 15, 226, 228, 474, 905; *imper.* 45, 311, 872, 907; *pres.1sg.* 51, 315, 396; **tellis** *pres.2sg.* 536; **tald** *pt.* 220, 403, 707; **tauld** 528, 727; *pp.* 905; **telland** *pres.p.* 560
tempest *n.* storm 15
ten *num.* ten 329, 440
tene *n.* anger 123, 457
tenefull *adj. as n.* enraged man 458
tent *n.* attention; *phrs.* **tak** ~ pay attention 314
teuch *adj.* hardy 521
tha see **thay** *demon.pl.*
thay *pron.* they 5 (1st use), 7, 8, 20 (1st use), 22 (2nd use), 24, etc; **thair** *poss.* 133, 208, 251, 349, 522, etc.; **þair** 271; **thame** *obj.* 220, 327, 331, 346, 351, etc.; **þame** *obj.* 271; themselves 831
thay *demon.pl.* (of 'that') those 2, 5 (2nd use), 20 (2nd use), 21, 22 (1st use), 35, 37, 187 (1st use), 350, 569, 654, 817, 821 (1st use), 829 (1st use), 951, 960; **tha** 748, 801
thair *adv.* there (in its various senses) 2, 19, 21, 30, 31, 42, etc.
thairfoir *adv.* therefore 202
thairin *adv.* in it 28, 650
thairof *adv.* on that account 418
thairtill *adv.* to it 110, 541
thairto *adv.* to that 562, 564, 845
thairun *adv.* on it 374
thairwithall *adv.* as a result 151
than *adv.*[1] than 62, 328, 430, 613, 668, etc.
than *adv.*[2] then 117, 131, 138, 278, 279, etc.
thank *n.* thanks 742
thank *v.imper.* thank (for) 79; *pres.1sg.* 946; **thankit** *pt.* 217, 271; *pp.* 852; **thankand** *pres.p.* 334, 338, 348
tharth *v. impers.* (I) need 535
that *rel.pron.* (those) who(m), which 6, 28, 72, 156, 170, 173, etc.; what 315, 380, 540
the, thy(n) *see* **thow**
thing *n.* matter, (sort of) behaviour 80, 481, 742; *pl.* matters 391
think *v.impers.* **me** ~ it seems to me 148, 214, 259, 434, 536; *phrs.* **as me** ~ **the** as it seems to me that you are 67, 73; **thocht** *pt.* 176; **the king** ~ **lang** it seemed tedious to the king 277
think *v.* to think, consider 848; **thocht** *pt.* 963

thir *demon.pl.* these 231, 283, 493, 560, 562, etc.; **this** 647, 661, 724
thyself *pron.* you 147, 630, 733, 753, 878, 896
thocht (that) *conj.* although 164, 236, 432, 522, 550, 661, 704
thocht *n.* thought, intention 911; *phrs.* **haue gude ~ on** remember 255; **had greit ~** took trouble/pains about 319, 364, 389
thocht *see* **think**
thopas *n.pl.* topazes 473n
thourtour *adj.* transverse, crosswise, separating 566
thousand *num.* thousand 327
thow *pron.2sg.* thou (familiar) 51, 54, 55, 62, 64, 70 (2x), etc.; **thy** *poss.* yours 45, 54n, 259; **thyne** 56; **þi** 241; **the** *obj.* 51, 59, 67, 73, 80, etc.; **thee** 248
thra *n.* haste, fury 800
thraly *adv.* eagerly, keenly 656, 700
thrawin *adj.* peevish, out of sorts 129
thre *num.* three 218, 339, 948
thre hundreth *num.* three hundred 756
threip *v.* to quarrel, contend 130, 911; *pres.pl.* 79, 197
threit *v.pt.* threatened, coerced 541
threit *n.* menace, threats; *phrs.* **with ~** belligerently *656n
threttie *num.* thirty 344, 693
thrife *v.* to prosper 53; **thriue** 129, 301; *phrs.* **sa mot I ~** *or* **sa ~ I** *lit.* may I have good luck, but generally rather empty 'indeed' 53, 129, 285, 449, 911
thring *v.* to press on, drive or cast 700; *pres.1sg.* ~ **doun** kill 197
thristit (in) *v.pt.* thrust, pressed (on) 656, 693, 700
throw *adv.* through 696
throw *prep.* through 656, 693, 700, 810
thus *adv.* consequently, thus 84, 173, 184, 203, 210, 569, etc.
thus-gaitis *adv.* in this manner *169n
ticht *v.pp.* tied 457, 473
tyde *n.* time, season 4, 48, 287
tyger *n.* tiger (emblem of ferocity) 457n
till *adv. prep.* until, to (sometimes postposited) 269, 316, 390, 451, 858
tyme *n.* time, period 1, 15, 439, 565, 798; *phrs.* **baith tyde and ~** continually, always 48
tyne *v.* to lose (one's life), perish 58, 823
tit *v.* to seize, pull about 432; **tyt** *pt.* 123
tyte *adv.* immediately 872, 907
tithyng *n.* tidings, news 581; **tythingis** *pl.* 960
to-blaisterit *v.pt.* scattered 28
today *adv.* today 376, 527, 880
togidder *adv.* together 251, 819; at one another 822
tomorne *adv.* tomorrow 85, 563

tonicht *adv.* tonight 237
tother *num.pron.adj.* **the** ~ (*representing* **that other**) the other 183
toun *n.* an enclosed settlement (ranging from a farmstead to a city like Paris) 349, 410, 790, 927; **town** 13
toun-man *n.* (*lit.* someone from an enclosed rural locale) villager, farmer 521
toworne *v.pp.* heavily worn, worn out 559
towsill *v.* handle roughly 432
traist *adj.* trustworthy, secure 546
traist *v.imper.* trust 308; **traistit (in)** *pt.* 391
trauale *n.* labour, toil, journey? 48; **trauaill** 244; **trauell** 950
trauelland *v.pres.p.* travelling, errant 872
trauellours *n.poss.* a wayfarer's 82
tre *n.* tree 457
treuth *n.* troth, fidelity 939
trew *adj.* true 546, 845
trewlie *adv.* truly 458
trewlufe *n.(pl.)* truelove knots, flower-like images 473n
trimland *v.pres.p.* trembling (in rage) 458
trystit *v.pp.* agreed, contracted 793
troublit *v.pp.* vexed, disturbed 136n
trow *v.* to trust, believe 876; *pres.1sg.* 56, 108, 316, 698, 884n; **trowis** *pres.2sg.* 538, 560; **trowit** *pt.* 604, 648
tuggil *v.* to wrestle, handle roughly 521
tuik, tuke *see* **ta**
turnit *v.pt.* changed course, set a course (towards) 4
twa *num.* two 43, 113, 123, 245, 365, 382, 418, 569, 613, 819, 865, 932
twentie *num.* twenty 357
twyse *adv.* twice, the second time 148

vmbekest *v.pt.* looked all round, surveyed completely 410
vnbraissit *v.pt.* undid, opened *628n
vnburely *adj.* inelegant, coarse 522, 695, 806
vncourtes *adj.* discourteous 122
vndeid *adj.* living, alive 854
vnderta *v.pres.1sg.* promise 241; **vndertuk** *pt.* *489n; **vndertuke** 529; **vndertane** *pp.* 364, 571
vndo *v.imper.* open 94
vneis *adv.* scarcely 155
vngane *v.pp.* not yet passed 660
vnkend *v.pp.* unknown 247
vnknawin *pp.adj.* unknown (here) or alien, ignorant (of how to) 127n
vnrufe *n.* (*lit.* lack of peace) trouble, disquiet 47
vnsemand *pp.adj.* unseemly, inappropriate 146

vnset *v.pp.* not yet seated 147
vnskilfull *adj.* unreasonable, uncouth 159
vnto *prep.* towards 5
vther *pron.adj.* second, other(s) 3, 72, 82, 114, 340, 391, 704, 820, 825, 927

vacant *n.* empty office or rank 757
vennysoun *n.* game generally (not necessarily deer) 208
vertew *n.* virtue 162
veseir *n.* visor 838
vincussing *n.* being vanquished 824n
voce *n.* voice 211

wa *adj.* disinclined, reluctant 247
wachis *n.pl.* guards, watchmen 274
way *adv.* away 434
way *n.* path, way 25, 30, 73, 326, 382, 397, 547, 595, 690, 797, 914; manner 566; **wayis** *pl.* 394, 586
wayndit *v.pt.* refrained, avoided 228
waird *n.* land-tenure (a specific kind of property holding) 759
wait *see* **wit**
waitis *v.pres.pl.* lay in wait for 912
wald *n.* hill, moorland 405
wald *see* **will**
walkand *v.pres.p.* walking 73, 106; *pt.* **walkit** 161
walkin *v.* to awaken 275; **walkinnit** *pt.* 280
wan *see* **win**
wanderand *v.pres.p.* wandering 328
wandit *v.pt.* tied, secured 366
wane *n.* dwelling-place, house, domain or territory 7, 190, 264, 366, 577, 629; **wanis** *pl.* 647, 689
wantis *v.pres.3sg.* lacks, is lacking 288; *pres.pl.* 970; **wantit** *pt.* 191, 266
wantoun *adj.* profligate, unrestrained 100
wappinis *n.pl.* weapons 515; **wapnis** 834
war *see* **be**
wardrop *n.* household department in charge of clothing and other domestic gear 239, 313, 379, 448
wardroparis *n.pl.* personal attendants 274
warysoun *n.* reward, payment, riches 915
warld *n.* world, worldly life 891
warrand *v.* to guarantee, swear 122, 159, 533, 586
was *see* **be**
wassalage *n.* (true) bravery or valour 886
watche *v.* to guard, keep watch 394, 405, 586
wed *v.* to marry 924

wedder *n.sg.* weather, storm 59, 97, 290; **wedderis** *pl.* 21, 27, 36, 74, 106, 283
weddit *v.pt.* married 958
weid *n.* clothing, garment, armour 576; **weidis** *pl.* 559
weild *v.* to govern, control (incl. a wife, esp. sexually) 924, 964; **weildit** *pt.* 577
weill *adv.* well 46, 83, 93, 249, 308, 394, 448, 484, 554, 579, 684, 704, 875
weir *n.*[1] *phrs.* **but/out of/foroutin ~; it worthis na ~** without doubt 228, 288, 499, 703
weir *n.*[2] war 460, 765, 823
weird *n.* fate, outcome 377
weit *adj.* wet 106
welcum *adv.* welcome 71; *adj.* 103, 179
wend, went *v.* to go, pass, turn aside 366, 629; **went** 690; **wend** *pres.1sg.* 249; **went** *pt.* 7, 9, 102, 186, 320, 354, 576, 605, 765, 824; *pt.subj.* 394; *pp.* 439, 725; *see also* **ga**
wene *v.pres.1sg.* think, expect 186; **wend** *pt.* 648
went *see* **wend**
weryouris *n.pl.* warriors 765, 788
weschin *see* **wosche**
wy *n.* warrior 577, 629, 648; **wyis** *pl.* 690
wicht *adj.* active, violent, valiant 36, 356, 753, 788, 964; **wythest** *super.* 765
wickit *adj.* evil, malign 21, 36, 106, 283, 891
widdeis *n.pl.* withies, strips of willow used as ties 366
wyde *adj.* broad, wide-stretching 2
wyfe *n.* wife, woman 133, 144, 157, 267, 924, 965; **wyfis** *poss.* 356
wyld *adj.* uncivilised, dangerous 161
wylit *v.pp. lit.* beguiled, tricked, deceived 708
will *adj.* lost, wandering 35, 73, 106; **willar** *comp.* 138
will *n.* desire, free will 540, 629, 764, 820, 890, 913, 939; **willis** *pl.* 502; *phrs.* **at thair will** as much as they might desire 208
will *v.pres.(subj.)* wish to, want to, to mark the future 55, 241, 252, 288, 290, 298, etc.; **wald** *pt.* 92, 392, 587, 603, 628, etc.; *pres.subj.* would wish 70, 226 (2x), 303, 394, 498, etc.
win *n.* joy 924
win *v.* to attain, approach, gain 110, 624; **wan** *pt.* 460, 764, 823; **win** *pp.adj.* won, gained 917
wind *n.* wind 16
wyne *n.* wine 186, 208, 266
wynning *n.* dwelling-place 227, 642
winnis *v.pres.3sg.* lives, dwells 527
wirk *v.* to work, act 377, 928; **wrocht** *pp.* prepared 264
wise *adj.* wise 356, 434; **wyse** 721, 726

wyse *n.* manner, way 433, 928
wyselie *adv.* carefully, prudently 586
wist *v.pt.* wished 21n
wit *v.* to know 226, 249, 642; **wait** *pres.* 46, 66, 262, 431, 448, 502, 520, 703; **wist** *pt.* 30; **wittin** *pp.* 603, 648
with *prep.* with (in its various senses, incl. the 'by' of agency, towards) 6, 7, 13, 43, 47, etc.
withall *adv.* in addition, also 659, 733, 830, 834
wythest *see* **wicht**
within *prep.* within, in 2, 188, 190, 354, 960
withoutin *prep.* without, discounting, excepting 44, 144, 149, 318, 340, etc.
with-thy *adv.* on the condition that 70
wonder *adv.* wondrously 24, 100, 247
wont *pp.adj.* accustomed 275, 577
word *n.* speech 100, 491, 514, 649, 689, 850, 946
worschip *n.* honour, renown, a position or office dependent on those qualities 460, 823, 964
worschipfull *adj.* honourable, splendid 576
worth *adj.* worth, to the value of 245
worthy *adj.* of worth/value, honourable (enough), noble (enough) 7, 624; **worthie** 66, 190, 292, 356, 461, 749, 963, 964; as *n.* worthy person 275, 764, 924; *pl.* noble men 725, 751; **worthiest** *super.* 9; *as n.* 143, 266; **worthyest** 186
worthie *adv.* worthily, honourably 360
worthylie *adv.* honourably 460
worthis *v.pres.3sg.* has become 691; is 703; **worthit** *pt.* became 830
wosche *v. pt.* washed 215; **weschin** *pp.* 143, 725
wox *v.pt.* grew, became 35, 100
wraith *adj.* angry 100
wraith *n.* anger 486
wrocht *see* **wirk**

yow *see* **ȝe**

ȝaip *adj.* active, vigorous 627
ȝair *adv.* attentively, carefully 640
ȝald *v,pt.* gave 224
ȝarne *adv.* eagerly 836
ȝe *pron.* you (plural and polite) 89, 103, 116, (addressing both Charles and Gyliane?)158, 179, 226, 284, 365, 908; **ȝhe** *370n; **ȝour** *poss.* 104, 881, 902; **ȝow** *obj.* 78, 114, 368, 371, 881, 901
ȝea *interj.* yes (emphatic), truly, indeed 298, 376, 544; **ȝe** 619
ȝeid *v.pt.* went 131, 267, 594
ȝeilding *n.* surrender 836

ȝeir *n.* year 200, 286, 756; *pl.* 661, 724; **ȝeiris** 231
ȝeman *n.* servant 627
ȝeme *v.imper.* take heed or pay attention 640
ȝet *n.* gate 608, 611, 627; **ȝettis** *pl.* 632
ȝit *adv.* yet, heretofore, still 80, 138, 169, 201, 253, 428, 658, 691
ȝone *demon.* that (for a 'distant' object, the first use perhaps derogatory) 367, 372, 703, 705, 780
Ȝule Christmas 251, 359; *phrs.* **the Ȝule-tyde** the Christmas season 4; **Ȝule-day** 286, 404; **Ȝule-nicht** Christmas Eve 342

Index of Proper Names